Essential Histories

The War of 1812

Essential Histories

The War of 1812

Carl Benn

First published in Great Britain in 2002 by Osprey Publishing,
Midland House, West Way, Botley, Oxford OX2 0PH, UK
44-02 23rd St, Suite 219, Long Island City, NY 11101, USA
Email: info@ospreypublishing.com

Osprey Publishing is part of the Osprey Group.

Transferred to digital print on demand 2010

First published 2002
7th impression 2008

Printed and bound by Cadmus Communications, USA

A CIP catalogue record for this book is available from the British Library

ISBN: 978 1 84176 466 5

Editorial by Kate Targett
Design by Ken Vail Graphic Design, Cambridge, UK
Cartography by The Map Studio
Index by Susan Williams
Picture research by Image Select International
Origination by Grasmere Digital Imaging, Leeds, UK

Acknowledgements
The author would like to thank fellow historians James Cheevers, Brian Leigh Dunnigan, Donald Hickey, Ty Martin, and
Gene Smith for their assistance; and to Donald E. Graves, who also undertook a much-appreciated critical reading of
the manuscript.

The Woodland Trust
Osprey Publishing is supporting the Woodland Trust, the UK's leading woodland conservation charity, by funding
the dedication of trees.

www.ospreypublishing.com

Contents

James Madison, President of the United States 1809–17,
depicted in a period print. (Library of Congress)

Introduction

Off the coast of Virginia in 1807, during Great Britain's long war with France, the captain of His Majesty's Ship *Leopard* ordered the United States frigate *Chesapeake* to stop so he could search it for deserters from the Royal Navy. The Americans refused. The British let loose a broadside that killed or wounded 21 men. After replying with a single artillery shot to assert the dignity of the flag, the *Chesapeake* surrendered, whereupon a boarding party seized four deserters on board the US vessel. This attack on a neutral warship outraged Americans, insulted their sovereignty, and served as a symbol of a wider crisis unfolding between Great Britain and the United States over free trade and sailors' rights.

Meanwhile, in the upper Mississippi Valley and western Great Lakes region, a Shawnee leader, Tecumseh, and his prophet brother, Tenskwatawa, spoke words of enraged bitterness and revitalization to the aboriginal peoples. Natives had lived through three decades of profound dislocation brought on by an expanding America that seemed to hold their rights in contempt if they conflicted with those of the land-hungry white population. Peaceful attempts to protect their interests had failed, and many tribal leaders now thought they had to go to war, as they had done in earlier times, to beat back the 'long knives' and secure a homeland for their children.

As relations degenerated towards war from 1807 to 1812, many Americans argued that the United States ought to seize the British provinces that lay to the north of the republic in order to get even with Britain, to realize America's destiny, or even to profit personally through territorial expansion. Others, such as President James Madison, desired conquest because these colonies were emerging as a competitor to the United States in the export of North American products. Annexation would benefit US expansion elsewhere too: in the west against the aboriginal tribes, who would be deprived of help from British officials and Canadian fur traders; and in the south, where filibusters and expansionists hoped that the subjugation of Canada would help them in realizing their goal of taking the Floridas from Britain's new European ally, Spain.

All these issues, along with a political crisis that threatened Madison's hold on power, came together in June 1812, when the United States declared war on Great Britain. A month later, US soldiers invaded Canada, heralding the onslaught of three years of war that would engulf the United States, Great Britain, its colonies, and many of the aboriginal nations of eastern North America.

In the following pages we will examine the War of 1812 on land and sea, study the still-debated causes and outcomes of the conflict, and explore some of the many interesting tales associated with the war.

Chronology

1793–1815 Anglo-French war, except briefly
in 1802–03, 1814–15

1806   November French Berlin Decree

1807   January/November British Orders-
in-Council
June HMS *Leopard* attacks
USS *Chesapeake*
December French Milan Decree
December US Embargo Act

1809   March US Non-Intercourse Act

1810   May US Macon's Bill Number Two
November French outwardly appear
to repeal their decrees

1811   March US imposes non-importation
on Britain
May USS *President* vs HMS *Little Belt*
September British Order-in-Council
restricts US–West Indian trade
November Battle of Tippecanoe
November US Congress begins to
debate war

1812   18 June US declares war
23 June Britain repeals Orders-in-
Council
23 June First naval encounter: escape
of HMS *Belvidera* from a US squadron
12 July American army invades
Canada from Detroit
16 July Skirmish at the Canard
Bridge
17 July Capture of Fort Mackinac
17 July Capture of USS *Nautilus* by a
Royal Navy (RN) squadron
5 August Engagement at Brownstown
9 August Engagement at Maguaga
13 August Capture of HMS *Alert* by
USS *Essex*

15 August Engagement at Fort
Dearborn
16 August Capture of Detroit
19 August USS *Constitution* vs HMS
Guerrière
3–16 September Siege of Fort
Harrison
5–9 September Action at Fort
Madison
5–12 September Siege of Fort Wayne
October RN begins blockading US
Atlantic coast
9 October Capture of HMS *Caledonia*,
HMS *Detroit* burned
12–13 October Battle of Queenston
Heights
18 October USS *Wasp* vs HMS *Frolic*
18 October Capture of USS *Wasp* and
Frolic by HMS *Poictiers*
25 October USS *United States* vs HMS
Macedonian
19–20 November Action at Lacolle
22 November HMS *Southampton* vs
USS *Vixen*
28 November Action at Red
House/Frenchman's Creek
17–18 December Engagement at
Mississenewa
29 December USS *Constitution* vs
HMS *Java*

1813   January RN blockades Chesapeake
and Delaware rivers
17 January Capture of USS *Viper* by
HMS *Narcissus*
22 January Battle of Frenchtown
(Raisin River)
February RN blockade extended
between the Delaware and
Chesapeake
February British begin raiding US
Atlantic coast
22 February Attack on Ogdensburg

24 February USS *Hornet* vs HMS *Peacock*

March RN blockade extended north to New York, south to Georgia

27 April Amphibious assault at York

28 April–9 May First siege of Fort Meigs

3 May Attack on Havre de Grace

25–27 May Amphibious assault at Fort George

29 May Amphibious assault at Sackett's Harbour

1 June HMS *Shannon* vs USS *Chesapeake*

3 June Capture of USS *Growler* and *Eagle*

6 June Battle of Stoney Creek

7 June Action at Forty Mile Creek

June–October Blockade of US-held Fort George

22 June Attack on Craney Island

24 June Attack on Hampton

24 June Battle of Beaver Dams

11 July Raid on Black Rock

21–28 July Second siege of Fort Meigs

29 July Raid at Burlington Beach

31 July Raid at Plattsburgh

31 July Raid on York

2 August Engagement at Fort Stephenson

6 August Occupation of Kent Island

7–10 August Engagement on Lake Ontario (Burlington Races)

14 August HMS *Pelican* vs USS *Argus*

3 September Americans burn and abandon Fort Madison

5 September USS *Enterprise* vs HMS *Boxer*

10 September Naval Battle of Put-in-Bay (Lake Erie)

5 October Battle of Moraviantown (Thames)

6 October Battle of Châteauguay

November RN blockade extended from New York to Narragansett Bay

1–2 November Action at French Creek

6 November Bombardment at Prescott

11 November Battle of Crysler's Farm

10–11 December Americans evacuate Fort George, burn Niagara and Queenston

19 December Capture of Fort Niagara

25 December Capture of USS *Vixen II* by HMS *Belvidera*

29–30 December Burning of Lewiston, Tuscarora, Fort Schlosser, Black Rock, Buffalo

1814 **16–24 January** Raids on Franklin County, NY

14 February Capture of HMS *Pictou* by USS *Constitution*

5 March Engagement at Longwoods

28 March HMS *Phoebe* and *Cherub* vs USS *Essex* and *Essex Junior*

30 March Action at Lacolle

20 April Capture of USS *Frolic* by HMS *Orpheus*

29 April USS *Peacock* vs HMS *Epervier*

May Napoleon abdicates; British resources freed for the American war

May RN blockade extended to New England

5–6 May Amphibious assault on Oswego

14–15 May Raid on Port Dover and other villages

30 May Engagement at Sandy Creek

2 June Occupation of Prairie du Chien

22 June Capture of USS *Rattlesnake* by HMS *Leander*

28 June USS *Wasp* vs HMS *Reindeer*

3 July Capture of Fort Erie

5 July Battle of Chippawa

11–12 July Occupation of Eastport

12 July Capture of USS *Syren* by HMS *Medway*

17–20 July Siege of Fort Shelby/Prairie du Chien

21 July Engagement at Campbell Island (Rock Island)

25 July Battle of Lundy's Lane

August Peace negotiations begin in Ghent

August–September Blockade of Fort Erie

2–3 August Battle of Conjocta Creek

4 August Battle of Mackinac Island

8 August Capture of USS *Somers* and *Ohio*

14 August HMS *Nancy* destroyed

14 August Assault on Fort Erie

22 August Skirmish at Pig Point

24 August Battle of Bladensburg; Washington occupied; navy yard burned

27–28 August Destruction of Fort Washington; occupation of Alexandria

August–September Actions against British squadron on the Potomac

1 September Occupation of Castine and Belfast

3 September Battle of Hampden

3–6 September Capture of USS *Tigress* and *Scorpion*

5 September Occupation of Bangor

5–6 September Battle of Rock Island Rapids (Credit Island)

7 September USS *Wasp vs* HMS *Avon*

10–11 September Occupation of Machias

11 September Battle of Plattsburgh

12 September Battle of North Point

13–14 September Bombardment of Fort McHenry

15 September Engagement at Fort Bowyer

15 September Sortie from Fort Erie

19 October Engagement at Cook's Mill

October–November Raids on the Lake Erie region of Upper Canada

5 November Americans evacuate and blow up Fort Erie, retire to Buffalo

December–January Hartford Convention

13–14 December Engagement on Lake Borgne

23–28 December Actions outside New Orleans and battle of Villeré Plantation

24 December Treaty negotiations conclude in Ghent

27 December Prince Regent ratifies Treaty of Ghent

1815   1 January Action outside New Orleans

8 January Battle of New Orleans

9–12 January Siege of Fort St Philip

14 January RN squadron *vs* USS *President*

11 February Capture of Fort Bowyer

16 February US ratifies Treaty of Ghent

20 February USS *Constitution vs* HMS *Levant* and *Cyane*

11 March Recapture of HMS *Levant* by an RN squadron

23 March USS *Hornet vs* HMS *Penguin*

24 May Skirmish at the Sink Hole

30 June USS *Peacock vs* East India Company Ship *Nautilus*

1815–16 Aboriginal tribes negotiate peace

A small war with complex causes

Sailors' rights

The *Chesapeake* affair symbolized how grave an issue 'impressment' was between Great Britain and the United States. The Royal Navy (RN) ratio of seamen per ton of ship was the smallest of the major maritime powers, and in its desperation to fill ships' companies in the war with France, it impressed men, a practice that amounted to little more than legalized kidnappings in port towns and from merchant vessels. Naturally, many victims deserted; as did other sailors who had volunteered for the RN but who later lamented their decision. Large numbers of these men fled to foreign ships, including American ones, for asylum and employment. At the same time, American and other foreign seamen, finding themselves down on their luck in some port far from home, joined the Royal Navy; often they also deserted.

All of these individuals, as well as Britons who had emigrated to the United States, were liable under British law to being seized for service in the navy. Consequently, the RN stopped merchant vessels to remove deserters, and they often also took US citizens and other individuals who had no history of prior service in the navy.

The number impressed is uncertain, but the United States issued a report stating that 6,057 men had been taken from American ships between 1803 and 1811. However, the list was full of duplications, and did not identify British-born sailors or individuals who had deserted from the RN after volunteering to serve.

Some officials also undermined the credibility of American claims of injustice by selling false citizenship documents, as happened in London, where one US diplomat provided certificates to deserters for a half-crown fee. Conversely, the British released illegally impressed people when their cases came to the attention of the authorities. Thus the issue was more complex than is commonly believed, but even with these ambiguities it nevertheless represented an affront to national sovereignty, and there can be no doubt that large numbers of Americans found themselves wrongly impressed.

When the *Leopard* fired on the *Chesapeake* and removed sailors (whom the US acknowledged were RN deserters), the tensions that had been brewing over impressment came to a head. Many Americans demanded a recourse to arms, asserting that it was one thing to take people from merchantmen, but quite another to attack a man-of-war. The British, desperate to prevent hostilities, repudiated the action, punished the officers responsible, and offered compensation. For his part, the American president, Thomas Jefferson, hoped to avoid a conflict, so the crisis passed, although passions continued to run high because impressment from merchant vessels did not stop.

At the same time, the United States Navy protected the country's neutrality whenever it could. On one occasion, in May 1811, the frigate USS *President* opened fire upon the smaller RN sloop *Little Belt*, which had been mistaken for a larger warship that had impressed some Americans. The sloop lost 32 killed and wounded, to only one person injured on the *President*. The US government apologized but exonerated the captain of the *President*. Nevertheless, the British did not pursue the matter because their attentions were focused on protecting themselves against Napoleon Bonaparte's dream of turning their island kingdom into a French vassal state.

This 1818 print shows Castle Williams in New York, built immediately after the *Chesapeake* affair of 1807. Coastal forts often had less artillery than the attacking squadrons, but shipboard guns were not as accurate because of the movement of the vessels. The earth or masonry walls of shore batteries could absorb shot better than wooden ships, and forts could return fire with heated shot to set vessels on fire. (National Maritime Museum)

Free trade

In addition to 'sailors' rights,' problems surrounding the issue of 'free trade' contributed to the American decision to go to war. As a neutral nation, the United States faced serious challenges in expanding its trade and gaining access to the world's markets while France and Britain made war against each other. Despite all this, US international trade actually grew dramatically before 1812, largely through opportunities created by these very wars. However, a watershed in the crisis occurred around 1805–07. Until that time, there had been problems enough: the United States had suffered from existing British and French restrictions, had fought the 'Quasi-War' of 1797–1801 with the French, and had seen hundreds of American ships seized by both European powers. Nevertheless, Britain essentially turned a blind eye to American ships that violated a British policy denying neutral vessels the right to replace belligerent ones in carrying goods between a belligerent's ports, so long as the Americans 'broke' the voyage by stopping in the US. (This then turned their cargo into 'American' exports.) In 1805, however, a British court decided that this was illegal, yet the British government decided not to enforce the decision, choosing instead to blockade part of the English Channel and North Sea but allow Americans to continue trading at non-blockaded ports.

Napoleon responded to the British actions with a series of decrees (beginning with the Berlin Decree of 1806). They were designed to destroy the economy of the United Kingdom by putting Britain under blockade and ordering the seizure of merchantmen – including American ones – carrying goods from the UK or its colonies. Bonaparte's

blockade was a sham because he could not enforce it, but the French did take large numbers of vessels entering their own ports and those of other European countries under French control. Britain retaliated with a series of Orders-in-Council, beginning in 1807. They declared all French and French-allied ports to be under blockade (which the RN only partially enforced) and ordered neutral ships apprehended unless (and as a concession) they put into British ports to pay duties on their cargoes. The objective was not so much to cut trade with France as to levy a tribute on merchants who traded with Britain's enemies. Napoleon responded with his Milan Decree in 1807, authorizing the confiscation of vessels that complied with the orders, and he later issued additional decrees to seize American ships that he claimed had violated either his own or US trade regulations.

Theoretically, both countries' policies were equally offensive to Americans, but Britain had the naval might to enforce them more effectively and hence became the focus of outrage. The US government rejected the authority of the decrees and the orders, arguing that blockades only could be lawful if fully enforced, which not even the Royal Navy could aspire to do. The Americans, however, did not want war, so they passed various laws themselves to restrict or halt trade with Britain, France, and, at one point, with the whole world. The thinking behind them was that European belligerents not only needed North American products to fight their wars, supply their manufacturers, and feed their people at home and in the West Indian colonies, but they also depended upon US merchant ships to move these goods – and European and colonial products – across the world's oceans. By restricting or denying access to these goods and services, the US would force the British and French to make the concessions America wanted, including further opening up the world's markets.

The most famous of the US laws was the Embargo of 1807, which fundamentally forbade trade with the entire world. It did not change London's views, but proved to be devastating to the US economy and

Eastern North America June 1812

RUPERT'S LAND

LOWER CANADA

UPPER CANADA

NEWFOUNDLAND

St John's

Lake Superior

INDIANA TERR.

ILLINOIS TERRITORY

Mackinac

Lake Huron

Ottawa

Quebec

NEW BRUNSWICK

PEI

Montreal

MASS (Maine)

Halifax

MICHIGAN TERRITORY

York

Lake Ontario

VT

NOVA SCOTIA

Lake Michigan

Detroit

Lake Erie

NEW YORK

Buffalo

NH

Boston

MISSOURI TERRITORY

MASS

CT   RI

INDIANA TERR.

OHIO

PENNSYLVANIA

NJ

New York

St Louis

Baltimore

Philadelphia

ATLANTIC OCEAN

Washington

MD

DEL

VIRGINIA

KENTUCKY

Mississippi

TENNESSEE

NORTH CAROLINA

SOUTH CAROLINA

MISSISSIPPI TERRITORY

GEORGIA

Charleston

Bermuda

Savannah

N

WEST FLORIDA

New Orleans

LOUISIANA

EAST FLORIDA

British territory

United States

Spanish territory

GULF OF MEXICO

BAHAMAS

Disputed territory between the US and Spain

0   250 miles

0   500 km

generated widespread opposition among Americans, who evaded its restrictions by smuggling goods across the porous border with British North America and through clandestine shipments from their own shores.

In 1809, James Madison succeeded Thomas Jefferson in the White House and replaced the Embargo with the milder Non-Intercourse Act. It prohibited trade with France and Britain, reopened commerce with other countries, and promised to resume relations with whichever belligerent changed its hurtful policies. This legislation also proved to be ineffective, and in 1810, it was replaced by Macon's Bill Number Two, which re-established trade with everyone but allowed the president to impose non-intercourse on one of the European powers if the other repealed its restrictions. Without any serious ability to blockade Britain, Napoleon offered to repeal his decrees if either the UK revoked the Orders-in-Council or the US imposed non-intercourse on Britain. At the same time, however, he issued a new decree that saw France actually seize more American vessels in 1810 than the Royal Navy did. Somehow the normally astute Madison either fell for the ploy or went along with it, and in November, he imposed non-intercourse on Britain. This delighted Bonaparte, who hoped for an Anglo-American confrontation to relieve some of the pressure the British were exerting against him, but he continued to take American vessels despite his promises.

The USS *President* vs HMS *Little Belt* in a contemporary print. (National Maritime Museum)

Expansionism

In 1810–11, the British did not think they could comply with American demands on impressment or trade, believing that the Royal Navy was their best weapon in the struggle against France and so had to be used as effectively as possible. This required the British to maintain its manpower levels. Furthermore, the impact of American restrictions, although injurious, was not sufficient to force concessions, and the British were strong enough that they could look beyond the immediate wartime crisis to the possibility that coercive measures might translate into an expansion of their own maritime economy, at the expense of their competitors, once peace had returned. Furthermore, when faced with the Embargo and similar actions, they sought out alternative sources of goods, and naturally

US Dragoon officer, painted in 1816. The British and Americans only had small numbers of cavalry during the War of 1812, which they used mainly for scouting, patrolling, and delivering dispatches, with mounted charges being rare. Cavalry normally wore more elaborate uniforms than the other branches of the military. (Houghton Library, Harvard University)

found that the British American colonies offered enormous potential to meet the needs of the Empire. Through preferential trade and other measures, London fostered that potential at a time when those colonies had developed to the point where they could produce valuable surpluses (spurred on in part by the vacuum created by American trade restrictions). Between 1807 and 1811, for instance, Canadian exports of pine and fir timber rose 556 percent. To strengthen the British provinces further at the expense of the United States, the British government issued an Order-in-Council in 1811 excluding American salted fish from the West Indian colonies and imposing heavy duties on other US imports. This was a blow to President Madison, who had assumed that the West Indies simply could not be fed without American fish, and thus it demonstrated the weakness of his trade policies as vehicles of coercion. At the same time, it underscored how much of a rival the British colonies had become, both in their own right and as a conduit for American smugglers seeking to avoid his restrictions.

Looking to the future, Madison worried that the Great Lakes-St Lawrence system through British territory even might turn out to be the main route that American goods from the northern interior would use to travel to Europe. The president therefore decided that those provinces had to be conquered. This would deny Britain access to North American produce entirely, except under conditions dictated by the United States (to say nothing of the impact annexation would have on the overall prosperity of the nation).

Many Americans supported expansion; for some, the expulsion of Britain from the continent represented a natural step in achieving the republic's destiny. Congressman John Harper articulated this idea in 1812, when he proclaimed that no less an authority than 'the Author of Nature' himself had 'marked our limits in the south, by the Gulf of Mexico [in what then was Spanish territory]; and on the north, by the regions of eternal frost.' For others, seizing Canada would be a fitting punishment to avenge their problems on the high seas.

Some leading expansionists wanted to profit personally from changing America's borders. Such were the aims of the entrepreneur and 'War Hawk' Peter B. Porter (who would command a brigade in the 1814 invasion of Canada). His views differed somewhat from Madison's because he thought both Upper and Lower Canada should be conquered but that only the upper province should be absorbed into the

American infantry, 1816, dressed in fundamental conformity to the tailoring requirement of the 1813 regulations, with minor variations that were typical of the era. Not all infantry wore the officially approved blue uniform; when scarcities of the correct cloth occurred, foot soldiers might find themselves sporting black, brown, or gray coats instead. (Houghton Library, Harvard University)

American union while the lower, largely francophone, colony should be turned into an independent state. This vision fitted with his business interests: on the one hand, he ran a carrying trade around Niagara Falls on the New York side of the border, and assumed that the conquest of Upper Canada would allow him to knock out or replace his competitors on the British side of the river; on the other hand, he did not want inland trade to move down the St Lawrence because he was a promoter of a canal system – the future Erie Canal – to move goods from the Great Lakes to the Hudson River and on to New York City. Having Lower Canada become a separate country would discourage the development of the St Lawrence route in order to keep the transportation system within the United States. It also would constrain entrepreneurs in Montreal and Quebec (who might compete against his interests) by ensuring their foreign status.

The Old Northwest

As debates over impressment, trade, and the destiny of British North America unfolded, other troubles on the western and southern frontiers helped to propel the United States to war. After the end of the American Revolution, in 1783, the aboriginal peoples in the Old Northwest (modern Ohio, Michigan, Indiana, and adjoining regions) saw a flood of hostile settlers stream into their territories. The newcomers not only wanted to take land, but the agricultural economy they brought with them changed the environment, as they cut down the forests, chased away the game, and rendered existing native subsistence patterns non viable. The mainly Algonkian-speaking peoples of the region (such as the Shawnees, Potawatomis, and Ottawas) responded to this challenge by forming a confederacy to fight for their homelands in the latter part of the 1780s; and at the battle of the Wabash in 1791, they inflicted the greatest defeat the US ever suffered at the hands of the natives. In 1794, however, the tribes lost the decisive battle of Fallen Timbers, and in 1795, surrendered most of Ohio and other tracts of land in return for a new boundary between themselves and the settlers. They hoped that an established border would allow them to evolve independently of unwanted intrusions in their remaining territories, but the lines proved to be temporary. Immediately after their creation, American authorities began to acquire more land through heavy-handed tactics, forcing the natives to continue moving west. In their desperation, the tribespeople again thought about uniting to defend their homes in the Old Northwest. In 1805, two Shawnee

brothers, the prophet Tenskwatawa and the political and military leader Tecumseh, began forming a pan-tribal confederacy. (Not all natives in the Great Lakes region were hostile to the US; some embraced neutrality, and small numbers of others allied themselves to the Americans.)

The British were implicated in the frontier crisis because the Crown had formed an alliance with the majority of tribespeople during the revolution and had supplied weapons and other assistance to them through the war years of the 1780s and 1790s. The British had hoped that native successes would allow them to help the tribes renegotiate the Anglo-American border of 1783 to create an aboriginal homeland on Upper Canada's south-western border, which, aside from the benefits it would provide to the tribes, would make the province more defensible. At the same time, Canadian fur traders moved freely through the region, conducting their business and helping maintain the British alliance.

As the clouds of war formed in the years before 1812, the British continued to cultivate native anger, recognizing that they would need aboriginal support to defend Canada. Yet they also tried to defuse frontier tensions in the hope of ultimately avoiding hostilities altogether. Naturally, their activities offended Americans, who were convinced that the British were plotting against them. These fears were only compounded by the first of the new round of battles for the frontier, when American forces clashed with the warriors of the western tribal confederacy at Tippecanoe in November 1811, some seven months before the outbreak of the Anglo-American war. This new crisis quickly amplified the cries for the conquest of Canada, to isolate the tribes from foreign aid and ensure that their opposition to American expansion could be more easily suppressed.

Far to the south, other expansionists thought that war against the natives and the conquest of Canada would help them achieve their own regional territorial ambitions. One of these 'prizes' was the land of the Creek nation, mainly within the Mississippi Territory, where tensions between natives and newcomers were similar to those in the Old Northwest. The Americans also wanted to annex the Spanish territories of East and West Florida. As it was, they had occupied much of West Florida before the outbreak of the War of 1812, but they assumed that hostilities with Spain's ally, Britain, would facilitate their designs on the remainder of these colonies.

Madison's political problems

The American declaration of war was also fuelled by James Madison's fears that he might lose the presidency in the election of late 1812. His perceived weakness in his handling of government in general, and of international affairs in particular, had generated widespread criticism and he faced the possibility of a challenger from within his own Democratic-Republican party, as well as Federalist Party opponents. (The Federalists advocated better relations with Britain over France.) The president thought he needed to take a stronger stand against the British in order to regain his party's confidence, which he assumed meant he had to either negotiate a settlement on American terms or go to war.

The negotiations that did take place were somewhat confused. Essentially, the British argued that revoking the Orders-in-Council would be wrong because Napoleon's actions had been fraudulent and therefore the US decision to invoke non-intercourse against the British made no sense, and even invited retaliation. Faced with factionalism within his own party, Madison would not admit to having made a mistake in accepting Bonaparte's offer because this would have confirmed the incompetence claimed by his political adversaries. He found himself in a corner in which the nation's interests and his own may have come into some conflict. With the realization that many leading supporters within his party opposed the continuation of ineffective trade policies, and in keeping with his developing annexationist views, Madison called Congress into an early session for November 1811 to prepare for war. His objectives were to unite his supporters and his critics and increase the pressure on the British to relent. If they did not, he would provide the country with the resources it would need to fight.

In the end, Madison embarked on a dubious war against Great Britain but skirted the challenges to his presidency, receiving his party's nomination in May 1812 and being reelected the following November.

'Free trade and sailor's rights' was not the simple cry of justice that popular history would have us believe. It was fraught with its own ambiguities and, perhaps more importantly, it was a cry co-opted to promote belligerency by annexationists who drove much of the government's thinking. Combined with the native crisis on the western border, and Madison's struggles to preserve his presidency, this led, in June 1812, to war. It was a small war when compared with the great conflict being fought over the European continent at the time, but nevertheless it was an important one in the histories of both North America and the British Empire.

Soldiers, sailors, and warriors

For a country contemplating war against the world's greatest naval power and against the tribes of the Old Northwest, the United States did not prepare well. In part, Americans were confident enough in their local superiority in North America to think that they did not need to invest heavily in their military, especially since Britain was not expected to be able to reinforce its colonies adequately because of the war in Europe. Many Americans also distrusted standing military forces, believing that a powerful army and navy might pose a threat to their own liberty; and they also possessed an unreasonable faith in the capabilities of the citizen militia. President Madison was typical of many in his discomfort with a professional military and of his embrace of the militia. Toward the end of the war, however, he realized his mistake first-hand when he witnessed the defeat of a force comprised largely of militia at the hands of British regular soldiers outside of Washington. 'I could never have believed that so great a difference existed between regular troops and a militia force, if I had not witnessed the scenes of this day,' he remarked.

Naval forces

Between the two branches of fighting service, the army and the navy, the United States Navy (USN) entered the conflict in better shape. With 7,250 sailors and marines in 1812, it was composed mainly of professional officers and experienced volunteer seamen, many of whom had seen action against the Barbary pirates of North Africa beginning in 1794 and in the Quasi-War with France of 1797–1801. Yet the navy suffered from inadequate funding and woolly political thinking in the prewar years, and thus was not as strong as it might have been by 1812. At the outbreak, the saltwater fleet had 13 operational vessels. Three of them were the famous 'super frigates,' *United States*, *Constitution*, and *President*; three were regular frigates; and, in descending order of size, there were five sloops and two brigs. There also were 165 coastal gunboats, 62 of

This plan from 1817 compares a British 38-gun frigate (top), armed principally with 18-pounder guns (firing 8kg balls) to an American 44-gun 'super frigate,' equipped primarily with 24-pounders (firing 11kg shot). (National Maritime Museum)

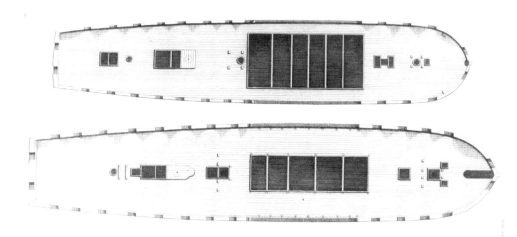

which were in commission. Of the vessels in reserve, the Americans repaired two frigates and cut down a third into a corvette in 1812–13. During the conflict, some captured British ships entered USN service and other vessels were built.

The Royal Navy was the world's most powerful maritime force, following Horatio Nelson's victory at Trafalgar in 1805. However, its size and successes masked serious problems. Most notably, France continued to pose a real threat at sea, which would prevent the RN from deploying significant resources to the western Atlantic unless and until the European situation improved (which the Americans did not expect to happen until they had conquered Canada, if indeed it happened at all). For instance, Napoleon only had 34 ships-of-the-line (main battleships) in 1807, having lost 30 in 1805–06, but he had increased that number to 80 by 1813 and had another 35 under construction. Meanwhile, Britain's ability to maintain equivalent vessels dropped from 113 to 98 between 1807 and 1814 as the years of war with France took their toll on the island kingdom of 12 million. In addition, the Royal Navy's global commitments forced it to send under-strength, ill-trained, and partially impressed crews to sea, often in badly built vessels. Yet in 1812, the sheer weight of the fleet promised to give the RN dominance in the western Atlantic, should Britain triumph over France.

Both sides also developed their freshwater capabilities on the Great Lakes and on Lake Champlain. The British entered the conflict with the advantage of their Provincial Marine, a transport service maintained by the army to move men and supplies in a region without adequate roads. It had two small ships and two schooners to serve Lake Ontario and the St Lawrence River as far down as Prescott, where the rapids shut off access to the rest of the river and the Atlantic beyond. To the west, on the other side of the great barrier at Niagara Falls, the Provincial Marine operated four vessels on Lake Erie, one of which had a shallow

enough draft to sail up the Detroit River to the upper Great Lakes. On Lake Champlain, however, a single derelict schooner protected British interests. At the outbreak of war, the Americans only had two gunboats on Lake Champlain, plus a brig on each of lakes Ontario and Erie. During the conflict, the two powers augmented their freshwater forces by taking merchant schooners into naval service, capturing enemy craft, and building new vessels at such a ferocious pace that historians have dubbed it 'The Shipbuilders' War.' For example, by August 1813, the British had increased their strength on Lake Ontario to six vessels carrying 97 guns and carronades, while the American squadron boasted 13 ships and schooners mounting 112 pieces of artillery.

Land forces

The land forces of the British and Americans in the war were fundamentally similar, although the Americans usually had a numerical advantage while the British had stronger leadership and better training. (The Americans did not begin to match these skills until the last year of hostilities.) Like other western armies, both the British and the Americans had a mix of line infantry, light infantry, artillery, and cavalry, along with various specialized troops, such as engineers. Both powers also relied heavily on part-time militiamen drawn from the civilian population. Indeed, the Americans would call out over 450,000 militia during the war, a number not much smaller than that of the total population of British North America. Additionally, both sides included elements which fell somewhere between the professionalism of the regulars and the amateurism of the militia, such as American volunteer corps and Canadian fencible regiments.

The land war was primarily an infantry struggle, fought by men organized into regimental or battalion formations that typically numbered 500–800 soldiers. The principal infantry firearm for both sides was the smoothbore, muzzle-loaded, single-shot, flintlock musket. Using paper cartridges containing a ball and powder (and sometimes extra buckshot, especially in American service), a soldier could load and fire his weapon two or three times each minute. In action, the musket could be reasonably accurate at 60 paces, and deadly at 175.[1] After that, its potency declined rapidly, to the point where there was little reason to fire at an enemy beyond 250 paces.

The most effective way of using muskets was to stand troops in tightly packed lines and fire massed volleys into the enemy at close range. Ideally, these volleys would shatter the enemy line so that the winning side could use its secondary weapon, the bayonet, to drive its adversaries from the field. There was some adaptation to the rough North American environment, such as thinning out the lines somewhat, but the fundamental principle of volley fire dominated the deployment and combat operations of both the United States and British armies.

As effective as these dense formations of infantry were – and it was these soldiers who would decide the big battles – they could not be used in all of the situations in which foot soldiers had to be engaged. Therefore, armies also needed light infantry soldiers if conditions called for skirmish and ambush skills and for guarding the line infantry's front, flanks, and rear. Normally, light infantry deployed in a very thin line, or chain, to allow their small numbers to cover a larger frontage than the formation they protected. This meant that they could not produce the volume of fire of line troops, which was their fundamental weakness. In battle, light infantry tried to preserve the main body from harassment by covering it so that it could approach the enemy in as fresh a state as possible. They might also try to harass the enemy line to blunt its fighting edge before the arrival of their own line. In retreat, light infantry might deploy to hold off pursuing troops long enough to allow the

main force to escape. In an advance, they might rush ahead to prevent the enemy recovering from a setback or to capture bridges and strong points.

Most light troops carried muskets, but some used rifles, which differed from muskets primarily in that their barrel

---

[1] A pace is about 30 inches (75cm).

interiors were not smooth but had spiral grooves cut into them; they were also intended to hold a tighter-fitting bullet. This meant that rifles could be more accurate than muskets and were dangerous at 350 paces or more. However, they took longer to load, fouled from gunpowder

The three men in this 1807 engraving would be expected to serve as warriors in native society. For battle, men often stripped down from the clothes seen here to their moccasins, leggings, breechcloths, and equipment. They also painted their bodies and prepared their hair in 'scalp locks,' which were often painted red and decorated with such spiritual objects as feathers and wampum. (National Archives of Canada)

Lieutenant's uniform of the rifle company of the Leeds Militia in
Upper Canada, 1812. Although most uniforms were flamboyant,
some light infantry uniforms were designed to make soldiers less
conspicuous because of the distinctive nature of their warfare.
(City of Toronto Museums and Heritage Services)

residue more quickly, and were limited by other problems. This prevented them from becoming the dominant infantry weapon until technological advances solved these issues in the middle of the 19th century.

In the confusion of popular history, a commonly held view is that the British fought, fundamentally, in tightly packed lines and the Americans deployed in a more individualistic manner and used cover, because of their experience on the North American continent. The reality was that it was the British who had proportionately more light infantry in their regular force in the War of 1812, and all armies in the western tradition had long recognized the need for a good balance of line and light troops.

Aboriginal forces

The populations of the aboriginal nations were too small and the life of each individual within a community of too great a value to allow for large numbers of casualties. Therefore, a fundamental principle of native warfare was to avoid losses, even to the point of giving up larger objectives to preserve lives in a war party. In addition, the personal freedoms enjoyed by members of native societies, combined with their conceptualizations of masculinity, meant that a warrior's participation in hostilities was voluntary. It depended upon his assessment of the opportunities available to him to win glory and prestige, and was sensitive to omens and signs that might lead him to withdraw from a campaign. These factors contributed to a style of native warfare distinct from white modes of fighting, resembling, at best, a kind of light infantry combat.

The main weapons carried by warriors were muskets, rifles, tomahawks, and knives, although spears, swords, and pistols were popular, and traditional clubs and bows still saw some use in 1812–15. Warriors preferred to ambush their adversaries or utilize other tactics that mimicked ambush in order to strike from an advantage, mask their movements to reduce casualties, upset their enemy's equilibrium, and thereby prevent the enemy from responding effectively. For example, a war party might conceal itself near a road until an enemy had passed, then attack from a position that blocked the line of retreat to demoralize its adversaries and thereby increase the odds of victory. Once engaged, natives often used war cries to try to unnerve their opponents further, and they kept up pressure by advancing in relays to prevent their foes from establishing a solid firing line. In a fixed firefight, warriors typically moved to a new position after each shot, so that an enemy would fire at a vacant spot (at least in theory) rather than one that was occupied. This was also designed to confuse their opponents about the size of the warrior force. If their enemies broke, the warriors gave chase, in the hope of killing and capturing as many of them as possible. If a war party had to retreat, it tried to minimize losses through a careful fighting withdrawal until it was out of harm's way.

Formidable as natives were in combat, they were not without their weaknesses. The threat of a high number of casualties could force them off a battlefield or even stop them from engaging in the first place. Their tactics also tended to work better in offensive rather than defensive engagements. Beyond these issues, natives took to the field not as pawns of the whites, but as allies, with their own goals, so their participation on campaign was conditional. Often British and American commanders failed to recognize this most basic of facts when they tried to have natives achieve some objective that did not meet aboriginal interests, and thus ended up complaining about the 'unreliability' of native war parties as they watched them withdraw from the field. For the Americans, however, especially in 1813 and 1814, their native allies provided them with their most effective light troops on the northern front, and for the British, aboriginals comprised a significant proportion of their forces in a conflict where the numerical odds were stacked against them.

America sets its sights on Canada

The declaration of war

On 5 November 1811, President James Madison delivered a message to Congress asking it to prepare for hostilities. Much of the ensuing debate was led by the War Hawks – mainly younger men from frontier regions who saw expansion, and the destruction of native resistance, as fundamental objectives for war, and who demanded a more aggressive approach to dealing with Great Britain than had been followed in previous years. In contrast, politicians who represented seaboard areas and shipping interests tended to oppose the slide toward belligerency. On 1 June 1812, Madison asked Congress to declare war, listing impressment, interference with trade, and British intrigue in the Old Northwest as causes, but remaining silent on the conquest of Canada because the point of the message was not to articulate objectives, but to blame Britain for hostilities. On 18 June, with votes of 79 to 49 in the House of Representatives and 19 to 13 in the Senate, the United States declared war on Great Britain.

In the final months of peace, the British had hoped to avoid a conflict that would see them trying to defend their colonies against heavy odds while they had their hands full in Europe. Furthermore, American trade restrictions, while not meeting Madison's objectives of bringing Britain to its knees, had hurt commercial interests in the United Kingdom and had generated calls for relief from its manufacturers and merchants. The problem lay in what concessions could be made. There was no reason to offer up territory, and British officials did not believe their activities among the tribes were so wrong because they considered them to be defensive in focus and because they worked

to keep a lid on frontier tensions so long as the United States restrained from hostilities. On the oceans, the Royal Navy's desperate manpower problems precluded relenting on impressment. What they could offer was the revocation of the Orders-in-Council, which they did on 16 June 1812. Nevertheless, word of this concession did not cross the Atlantic until after the United States had declared war, and it was not enough to inspire Madison to stop fighting.

The strategic situation

Americans confidently predicted that the conquest of Canada would occur quickly, if not painlessly. In August 1812, Thomas Jefferson wrote: '... the acquisition of Canada this year as far as the neighbourhood of Quebec, will be a mere matter of marching and will give us experience for the attack on Halifax the next, and the final expulsion of England from the American continent.' The *National Intelligencer* published an article in December 1811 expressing the Madison administration's view that the whole of Canada west of Quebec was 'in the power of the U. States because it consists of a long and slender chain of settlers unable to succour or protect each other, and separated only by a narrow water from a populous and powerful part of the Union,' while the fortified city of Quebec itself could be reduced through siege. All that would be needed, according to the newspaper, was an army of 20,000, only one-third of which needed to be regulars.

There were good reasons for the Americans to feel confident. All of British North America had only a half-million people, compared to 7.5 million for the United States, while the front-line province of Upper Canada was particularly vulnerable, with a population of 70–80,000. Many of these people were loyalists who had moved north as refugees from the American Revolution or their children, who might be expected to stand firm. However, many more settlers were recent American immigrants who had been attracted to the province because they could acquire their own land more easily than they could on the American frontier but who might not be hostile to annexation. This possibility was not lost on the British commander in Upper Canada, Isaac Brock, who thought it might be unwise to arm more than 4,000 of the 11,000 men of the militia. In Lower Canada, the majority were French-Canadians, whose ancestors had been conquered by the British in 1763 and who had shown only limited support for the Crown during the American Revolution. While their language, religious, and other rights were protected under British law, officials doubted that they would rally with enthusiasm to repel an invasion. The Atlantic provinces were more homogeneously British and were more isolated from attack, so the odds of their surviving seemed greater than in the Canadas.

Another card that seemed to play into the hands of the Americans was the state of the aboriginal population of the Canadas. Unlike those on the American frontier who followed Tecumseh and Tenskwatawa, these natives were undecided about what to do. Many assumed that the Americans would overwhelm the provinces and thus did not want to be punished for fighting on the losing side. Others were unhappy about how they had been treated by the Crown in the years leading up to 1812 over such issues as the alienation of land and the amount of independence they could exercise within the colony, so they had reasons to hold back when government officials tried to obtain their assistance. The internal aboriginal situation was so uncertain that the British were afraid that the tribes near the border might actually join the Americans once an invasion

occurred to buy peace with them. This would discourage militiamen from leaving their families unguarded to meet broader strategic objectives and might pose an insurmountable challenge to the small force of regulars in the colony.

In contrast to the natives of the lower Great Lakes, however, those within the British areas of the upper lakes had closer ties to the fur trade community, and officials assumed that at worst they would adopt a position of neutrality, but that there was a good possibility of encouraging them to oppose the Americans.

Another major reason why American leaders expected to conquer the British provinces easily was that the garrison in Upper and Lower Canada numbered only 7,000 soldiers in 1812 and could not be reinforced significantly while Napoleon menaced Britain. Furthermore, these troops needed to be concentrated to guard Montreal and Quebec. Montreal had to be maintained in order to keep the St Lawrence River open so that troops and supplies could be moved to the upper province; otherwise, that colony would be doomed. However, if Montreal could not be held, the troops deployed around it had to be able to retreat to Quebec, the strongest position in British North America. This had to be held, in the hope that a relief force, if available, could cross the Atlantic and rescue it before trying to recover lost territory up the St Lawrence River and into the Great Lakes region. This strategy, logical as it was, meant that Upper Canada, the more vulnerable colony, entered the war defended by only 1,600 regulars.

Yet the US army was not as formidable as was commonly believed. At the outbreak, it had an authorized strength of 35,600, but only 13,000 soldiers actually had been enlisted, and many of them were untrained recruits. Nevertheless, a concentrated blow against the upper province could be decisive, and as the conflict wore on, the Americans appeared to possess the capacity to increase the disparities in numbers dramatically and quickly.

Opening moves

On 4 April 1812, the United States implemented an embargo on international trade in order to get its merchant ships into American ports and prevent them from falling into British hands. At the outbreak of hostilities in mid-June, a squadron of five warships sailed from New York in anticipation of capturing an important merchant convoy, but became diverted on 23 June when it sighted the British frigate *Belvidera*. Her captain was suspicious enough not to let his guard down, and fled north as soon as the Americans opened fire. The Americans gave chase, and both sides inflicted casualties, but the *Belvidera* escaped to Halifax, saving the British commercial fleet in the process by diverting the Americans, and heralded the coming of war. The commodore at Halifax took his ships to sea in pursuit of the US squadron.

At about the same time, the American privateer *Dash* spotted a small Royal Navy schooner, the *Whiting*, lying at anchor in Hampton Roads, and quickly overwhelmed her crew, who were unaware that war had been declared, and were in fact on a mission to deliver diplomatic dispatches. The US government released the *Whiting*, but she did not make it back to England, being captured on the way by a French privateer,

symbolizing how Britain now had to fight two distinct but overlapping wars. (Rarely, however, would the Americans and French cooperate against their common enemy. One exception occurred in 1814, when the British frigate HMS *Majestic* beat off two French frigates, an American privateer, and other craft, capturing an enemy frigate in the process.)

On the northern front, the Americans put their armies in motion to make a simultaneous three- or four-pronged invasion of Canada across the Detroit, Niagara, and St Lawrence rivers, as well as against Montreal. The plan promised to divide the outnumbered defenders, thereby increasing the odds against them, and with the taking of Montreal, guarantee the fall of Upper Canada. However, the US army, led largely by over-the-hill political appointees and without a proper staff or adequate supply system, could not pull off the plan. Instead, the invasions came piecemeal over several months, the first occurring in July, when Brigadier-General William Hull led his force across the Detroit River into Upper Canada.

Halifax was the main Royal Navy station in British North America. The guns in this 1801 image are mounted on traversing carriages to maximize their field of fire. (National Archives of Canada)

The war on land and at sea

The Great Lakes –St Lawrence front

Most of the fighting in the War of 1812 occurred along the upper St Lawrence River and through the Great Lakes region because the conquest of British territory was the primary military objective of the United States.

America's other main territorial ambition in the war – the elimination of the western tribes as a roadblock to expansion – assumed that the fall of Canada would deprive natives of the trade, diplomatic, and military alliances that they needed to protect their interests.

As a result, American forces crossed into Canada in each of 1812, 1813, and 1814, bent on conquest, and won a number of important, even legendary, victories. Yet in only one of the eight invasion attempts did they achieve their objective of occupying British territory for more than a short (and contested) period; and that land, in south-western Upper Canada, was later handed back in the peace treaty.

Britain countered with land and sea offensives, directed from Canada and along the Atlantic and Gulf coasts of the United States. These efforts were designed, fundamentally, to cripple the ability of America to threaten the British colonies and to force an end to the conflict, as well as to avenge the suffering experienced by the Canadian population. If the British also managed to occupy some American territory in the process, then they thought the international border might be redrawn to make Canada more defensible, especially if a native homeland could be carved out of the Old Northwest. Nonetheless, their primary objective was to retain Canada, and the war for the British was essentially defensive.

1812

When William Hull's army crossed into Canada on 12 July, the senior officer in Upper Canada, Major-General Isaac Brock, sought to strike back at the invaders with energy. He believed he had to take bold action to reassure the settler population and demonstrate British strength to the aboriginal people, whose help he would need if the upper province were to have any chance of survival.

Fortunately for Brock, Hull's invasion began to falter almost as soon as it had begun. Instead of marching on the fort at Amherstburg to knock the British out of the Detroit region and intimidate the natives and settlers into submission, a nervous Hull dithered, engaged in some minor skirmishing, and worried that his army might be too weak to achieve its objectives. (Only one of his four regiments consisted of regulars; the others were militiamen.) In addition, on Lake Erie, the British captured a vessel carrying Hull's baggage, medical supplies, and important papers, which made him feel more vulnerable since his overland supply line ran through dismal swamplands threatened by Tecumseh's followers.

Meanwhile, to the north, on Brock's orders, soldiers, fur traders, and native warriors captured the American fort on Mackinac Island on 17 July without a fight, after quietly mounting an artillery piece overlooking the unsuspecting post and then demanding its surrender.

This bloodless victory was significant because it secured the important British fur trade operations in the north from a local American threat and helped to preserve southward connections through Lake Michigan to the tribes of the Mississippi region. It also inspired a good portion of the natives of the upper lakes to take up arms against the United States.

The Canadian front 1812–14

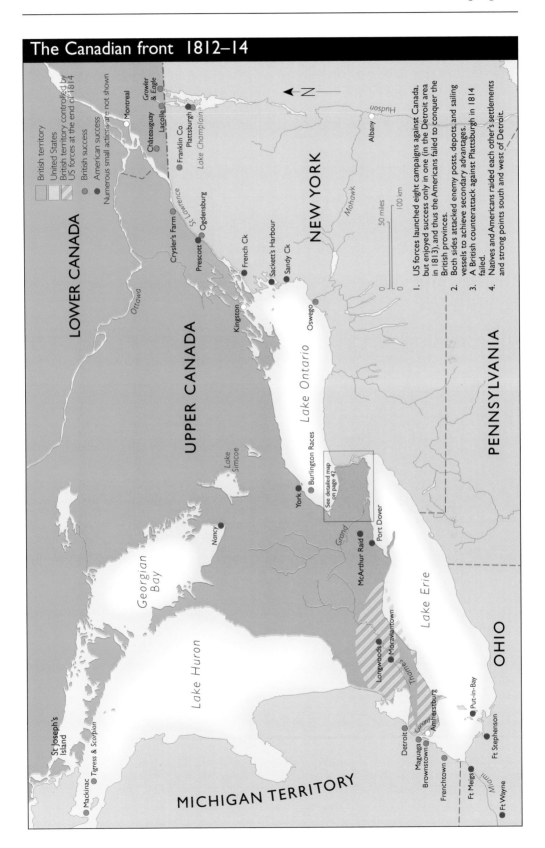

Legend:
- British territory
- United States
- British territory controlled by US forces at the end of 1814
- British success
- American success
- Numerous small actions are not shown

LOWER CANADA

UPPER CANADA

NEW YORK

PENNSYLVANIA

OHIO

MICHIGAN TERRITORY

Montreal
Chateauguay
Lacolle
Growler & Eagle
Franklin Co
Plattsburgh
Lake Champlain
Albany
Hudson
Mohawk
St Lawrence
Crysler's Farm
Prescott
Ogdensburg
French Ck
Sackett's Harbour
Sandy Ck
Kingston
Oswego
Ottawa
Lake Ontario
Lake Simcoe
York
Burlington Races
See detailed map on page 42
Nancy
Grand
McArthur Raid
Port Dover
Georgian Bay
Lake Huron
St Joseph's Island
Mackinac
Tigress & Scorpion
Longwoods
Moraviantown
Thames
Lake Erie
Put-in-Bay
Amherstburg
Detroit
Maguaga
Brownstown
Frenchtown
Ft Meigs
Miami
Ft Wayne
Ft Stephenson

0   50 miles
0   100 km

1. US forces launched eight campaigns against Canada, but enjoyed success only in one (in the Detroit area in 1813), and thus the Americans failed to conquer the British provinces.
2. Both sides attacked enemy posts, depots, and sailing vessels to achieve secondary advantages.
3. A British counterattack against Plattsburgh in 1814 failed.
4. Natives and Americans raided each other's settlements and strong points south and west of Detroit.

See detailed map on page 42

When Hull learned about the loss of Mackinac, he assumed that the tribes along the Detroit border would rise against him and perhaps fall upon the settlers on the American frontier. Therefore, on 8 August, he withdrew most of his men from Canada to secure his army inside Detroit, sent a plea for reinforcements so he could resume the offensive, and also ordered the garrison at Fort Dearborn (now Chicago) to withdraw, in anticipation of widespread aboriginal hostilities. At the same time, he learned that the campaign against Montreal, designed in part to divide British forces and assist his efforts, had been postponed. Closer to home, Hull received further frightening news that the western tribes had attacked a supply column on its way to Detroit at Brownstown

and had beaten off a force sent to meet it. He dispatched 600 men south to reopen communications, but British and native forces ambushed it at Maguaga on 9 August. The Americans did repulse the attack, but they failed to achieve their objective and suffered heavy casualties. As they retired to Detroit, the British Provincial Marine demonstrated its mastery on Lake Erie by subjecting them to a barrage along those parts of the road that ran past the shoreline. Now thoroughly demoralized, on 11 August, Hull pulled his remaining troops out of Canada, and a few days later, a

Mackinac, from an 1813 print, with the fur trade community in the foreground and the garrison behind. (William L. Clements Library)

Potawatomi force destroyed the garrison at Fort Dearborn as it complied with Hull's orders to evacuate that post.

Isaac Brock arrived on the Detroit River from Niagara on 13 August. Two days later, he demanded William Hull's surrender and tried to unnerve him by threatening massacre: 'It is far from my intention to join in a war of extermination,' he wrote, 'but you must be aware, that the numerous body of Indians who have attached themselves to my troops will be beyond control the moment the contest commences.' Hull still had enough nerve to reject the summons, and perhaps was wise enough to realize that the threat probably was an empty one, but after a cross-river artillery bombardment on the night of 15/16 August, followed by a British advance against the settlement, his resolve disappeared. Before Brock's men could get within range of the town, Hull lowered the Stars and Stripes over Detroit. To a mixed force of 1,300 regulars, militia, and natives, Hull surrendered 2,200 men, large quantities of weapons and supplies, the USN brig on Lake Erie, and the whole of the Michigan Territory.

This was a critical victory for Brock. He had secured his western flank, acquired desperately needed equipment for his poorly armed militia, and sent a powerful signal to bolster the faithful, encourage the wavering, and subdue the disloyal in both the white and native populations of Upper Canada. Most of the Iroquois of the Six Nations Tract along the Grand River, for instance, who had largely stood aloof before the capture of Detroit, swung behind the British, adding 400 valuable warriors to augment the Upper Canadian garrison.

With the approach of autumn, the Americans next mustered several thousand regulars, volunteers, and militia along the Niagara River for a second invasion of Upper Canada. Their plan was to cut the province in half, seize superior winter quarters, demoralize the population, and wipe away the disgrace of Hull's surrender. However, they suffered from poor training, bad equipment, inadequate supplies, and a deep

Mohawk chief John Norton (depicted in an 1805 miniature) commanded the Six Nations Iroquois at Queenston Heights. During the early stages of the battle, when his warriors kept the Americans from consolidating their position, his men 'returned the Fire of the Enemy with coolness & Spirit, – and altho' their fire certainly made the greatest noise, from the Number of Musquets, yet I believe ours did the most Execution.' Across the battlefield, volunteer rifleman Jared Willson thought 'hell had broken loose and let her dogs of war upon us. In short, I expected every moment to be made a "cold Yanky" as the soldier says.' (National Archives of Canada)

tension between the senior officers – Brigadier-General Alexander Smyth of the army and Major-General Stephen Van Rensselaer of the New York Militia. Consequently, when Van Rensselaer's men crossed the border, most of Smyth's troops sat out the confrontation.

The thrust came on the night of 12/13 October 1812. Batteries along the length of the Niagara River opened fire on British positions while Van Rensselaer's troops rowed across the waterway from Lewiston to Queenston. As they got out into the current, they came under fire and suffered heavily. Yet they persevered, reached the Canadian shore, secured their landing, and found a way to the top of Queenston Heights, a natural ridge that dominated the village of Queenston and the surrounding countryside. General Brock counterattacked, leading an outnumbered British and Canadian force up the steep heights in a frontal charge. The American line opened fire, Brock fell mortally wounded, and the charge faltered shortly afterward.

Brock's successor, Major-General Roger Sheaffe, ordered more troops and Iroquois warriors to converge on Queenston from Fort George in the north and from posts to the south. At the same time, small detachments of British soldiers at the landing kept the Americans out of the village of Queenston and continued to harass the boats ferrying men and supplies across the border. The Iroquois were the first reinforcements to arrive on the scene. They ascended the heights inland, out of range and sight of the Americans, then attacked from behind the cover of the forest and scrub. Although badly outnumbered, the warriors managed to keep their ill-trained enemy pinned down in open ground close to the riverside cliff of the heights. One key factor in their success was the absence of sufficient numbers of competent American light infantry to drive the tribesmen away from the US line standing exposed in the open. Thus the Americans fired heavy but ineffectual volleys at the warriors in the brush to their front, while the Six Nations returned fire with far fewer shots, but with more effect.

Iroquois efforts enabled Sheaffe to assemble 900 regulars, militia, volunteers, and additional warriors on top of the heights out of range of his enemy. He then led them across flat ground against American soldiers who had been badly shaken by the natives, had expended much of their ammunition, and who felt trapped because their compatriots – frightened by the aboriginal presence and British fire – refused to row back across the river, either to reinforce or to rescue them. Sheaffe's force marched forward, fired one volley, and charged.

Within 15 minutes it was over. The Americans had suffered another humiliation, losing as many as 500 killed and wounded and 960 prisoners-of-war. On the British side, there were only 104 killed and wounded. Within a week, another 1,000 dismayed American fighting men had deserted their camps on the New York side of the border and headed for home.

In November, Alexander Smyth led another US thrust across the Niagara River, near Fort Erie, at Red House and Frenchman's Creek, but cancelled the invasion shortly after encountering stiff British and native opposition. To the east, American forces made two half-hearted attempts against Montreal from Plattsburgh, but withdrew when they encountered resistance from defending forces.

The outcome of the 1812 Detroit, Niagara, and Montreal campaigns was not the one Americans had expected. The United States had lost every engagement of significance and had suffered huge losses in prestige, supplies, land, and men in proportion to the resources their opponents had applied in defending their territory. The British had even occupied sufficient American territory to allow many in the western tribal confederacy, as well as their British and Canadian friends, to think that the dream of an independent indigenous homeland might be achieved.

1813

Great Britain and the United States both took measures to increase their forces along the Canadian-American border over the winter of 1812/13, in anticipation of the second season's fighting. Despite their European commitments, the British managed to spare five additional infantry battalions, part of a cavalry regiment, and other reinforcements for the American war. Within the Canadian colonies, some militiamen were incorporated for full-time service and a few special units, such as the Provincial Dragoons, were raised. The Royal Navy took command of the Provincial Marine and added 470 officers and ratings to the

Some Americans thought the army should equip one-third of each infantry regiment with pikes (and shortened muskets slung over the pikemen's backs) because in close combat the extra reach of the pike would give the Americans a decided advantage over enemies using bayonets on the end of their muskets. However, the idea was not popular, and the only regiment that may have adopted the idea was the 15th Infantry during the advance against Montreal in 1812 and in the battle of York in 1813. Both navies, however, used pikes. For example, 200 British sailors at the amphibious attack on Oswego in 1814 carried them. This print is from *The American military library*, published in 1809. (Library of Congress)

freshwater ships, along with carpenters to build up the Great Lakes squadrons. In the United States, Congress authorized 20 new infantry regiments, approved an expansion of the navy, and sent hundreds of sailors to the Great Lakes from the Atlantic, where a developing British blockade of the eastern seaboard prevented much of the saltwater fleet from setting sail.

The first battle of 1813 occurred in the Detroit region, following several months of minor hostilities in which Americans and natives attacked each other's strong points and villages south and west of Lake Erie. The US sent an army to assert control in this contested area and to retake the territory that had been lost in 1812, but its advanced guard suffered defeat at Frenchtown (now Monroe) in the January snows at the hands of Brigadier-General Henry Procter. To the east, on 22 February, the British captured Ogdensburg in an effort to weaken the American threats to the St Lawrence lifeline that connected Upper Canada to the rest of the British Empire.

Meanwhile, in Washington, Secretary of War John Armstrong spent the winter planning a new strategy for the invasion of British territory. He thought the first target should be Kingston, and the naval squadron anchored there, because the British would not be able to hold Upper Canada if they lost their warships on Lake Ontario. However, the American commanders on the northern front – Major-General Henry Dearborn of the army and Commodore Isaac Chauncey of the navy – did not want to attack Kingston because they overestimated the strength of its fortifications. Instead, they thought that the more weakly defended York (now Toronto) should be seized. They argued that the capture of two warships in the town would swing the balance of power on Lake Ontario to the United States and facilitate the second and third phases of their proposed plan – the capture of the Niagara Peninsula, followed by offensive operations against either Kingston or Montreal late in the year. At first, Washington rejected the scheme, realizing that Armstrong's was the better strategy, but the federal government eventually accepted it for political reasons. The pro-war governor of New York, Daniel Tompkins, was seeking reelection in April 1813 but feared defeat through voter disenchantment with the lack of progress of the war. Thus a victory on the Canadian front was needed to help swing voters over to Tompkins. York was a good target because of its vulnerability and because its capture would have good propaganda value since it was the capital of Canada.

The Americans sailed from Sackett's Harbour, at the south-east corner of Lake Ontario, and on 27 April, launched an amphibious assault against the town of York. They drove General Sheaffe out of the capital and seized a large quantity of supplies. However, they did not get the British ships:

The battle of York ended when the British retreated from their fortifications and blew up a magazine full of gunpowder, inflicting 250 casualties upon the Americans in the explosion. Among those mortally wounded was US Brigadier-General Zebulon Pike, depicted in this c.1815 print. One witness to the blast said that he 'felt a tremulous motion in the earth resembling the shock of an earthquake, and looking toward the spot ... saw an immense cloud ascend into the air ... At first it was a great confused mass of smoke, timber, men, earth, &c., but as it rose in a most majestic manner it assumed the shape of a vast balloon.' (National Archives of Canada)

one had left shortly before the attack, and the British had burned the other before retreating. Through delays brought on by bad weather, the battle actually took place too late to have a legitimate influence on the election; however, Tompkins' supporters simply circulated victory proclamations to an unsuspecting electorate before the assault occurred and Dearborn kept the New York troops in his army at home to vote for the governor, with the result that he squeaked back into power by 3,606 votes. The Americans occupied York for a week, and then returned to Sackett's Harbour, before implementing the second phase of the Dearborn-Chauncey plan.

On 25 May, the guns of Fort Niagara and the US Lake Ontario squadron began a two-day bombardment of Fort George at the mouth of the Niagara River. On 27 May, the American army landed near the

This early 19th century print shows a corner of the American Fort Niagara at the mouth of the Niagara River in the right foreground. In the left background is British Fort George with its naval station by the waterfront. In reality they were further apart than depicted here, but were well within range of each other's artillery. (National Archives of Canada)

now-destroyed fort. About 1,000 soldiers, militiamen, and warriors met the 4–5,000 Americans, but were repulsed after losing one-third of their force in the fighting. Defeated, they abandoned not only Fort George but also Fort Erie and the other posts along the Niagara River to retreat to Burlington Heights (now Hamilton). So far, the plan seemed to be working as US forces occupied the former British posts and rebuilt Fort George to secure their Upper Canadian toehold. At that point, the province was on the brink of being cut in half, with Procter's and Tecumseh's forces to the west facing the possibility of their already poor supply lines being severed completely. As it was, the retreat from Fort Erie had allowed the Americans to sail naval vessels, previously trapped by British artillery on the Niagara River, west to join the squadron being built on Lake Erie that would challenge the Royal Navy later that year. In addition, an attempt by the British to destroy Sackett's Harbour while the USN squadron was away at the western end of Lake Ontario failed on 29 May, further demoralizing Upper Canada's defenders.

On the Niagara Peninsula, General Dearborn followed up his success at Fort George by sending an expedition to knock the British out of Burlington Heights and force them to retreat to Kingston. Dearborn's thinking was influenced in part by information that the Grand River Iroquois were worried that the Americans might make a punitive attack against their settlements since there was now nothing to prevent them from such a strike. Concerned to preserve their territory, the Six Nations considered abandoning the British and buying American forgiveness by falling upon the redcoats if they retreated eastward. Thus, as Dearborn dispatched 3,700 infantry, artillery, and cavalry toward Burlington, Iroquois warriors assembled near the British camp but, with the exception of a handful of men, refused to

have anything to do with the redcoats when Crown officials tried to secure their help. On 5 June, the Americans camped at Stoney Creek for the night to rest before the assault.

Recognizing the combined American and aboriginal threats and worrying about the fate of the Canadian population, the British made a desperate decision. Rather than await the Americans, they would launch a surprise attack against their enemy with 700 men at 2.00 a.m. on 6 June. The ensuing battle of Stoney Creek was a violent and confused affair: friend shot at friend, and the two American brigadier-generals walked into the hands of British troops because they could not distinguish blue from red uniforms in the dark. After sharp fighting, the British withdrew, but they had achieved their objective because their enemies cancelled their plans and retired to a camp on the Lake Ontario shoreline at Forty Mile Creek. The Grand River people, although still nervous, cautiously decided to maintain their alliance with the British, which quickly solidified as events unfolded over the following weeks.

Sackett's Harbour (as represented in an 1815 print) was the main American naval base on Lake Ontario. (US Naval Historical Center)

A short time later, a small party of pro-British Iroquois ambushed an American patrol and chased it into the camp at Forty Mile Creek. At about the same time, the Royal Navy squadron, which had sailed west from Kingston to support the army, bombarded the site. Although both acts were fundamentally ineffective, the Americans abandoned much of their equipment and fled to Fort George, with native warriors and Canadian militia pursuing them to capture stragglers and supplies. General Dearborn assumed that the British were about to launch a counteroffensive, so he evacuated all of the newly won positions except Fort George. The British, under the command of Major-General John Vincent, reoccupied the vacant posts and began to put pressure on Fort George. At the same time, additional aboriginal reinforcements from Iroquois and Algonkian communities in Lower Canada arrived, followed by more warriors from the west and the north, until Vincent had over 800 tribesmen in his lines. Combined with his own troops, he was well equipped to annoy the Americans.

Dearborn responded to the developing challenge by organizing a secret expedition to destroy an important forward British position near Beaver Dams. About 600 infantry, cavalry, and artillery moved from Fort George south toward Queenston before swinging inland against the target, in an effort to confuse his opponents as to the destination. However, a Canadian, Laura Secord, overheard American officers discussing their plan and rushed off to warn the British, who detached men to watch the various routes along which their enemy might come. As the column continued its march, aboriginal scouts spotted it and alerted a native force of 465 that had been deployed along one of the roads. The tribesmen ambushed the soldiers on 24 June. As at Queenston, the Americans suffered from inadequate light infantry, and despite holding their own for three hours in the fierce battle, they surrendered, having suffered 100 casualties, compared to 50 on the native side.

The Niagara front 1812–14

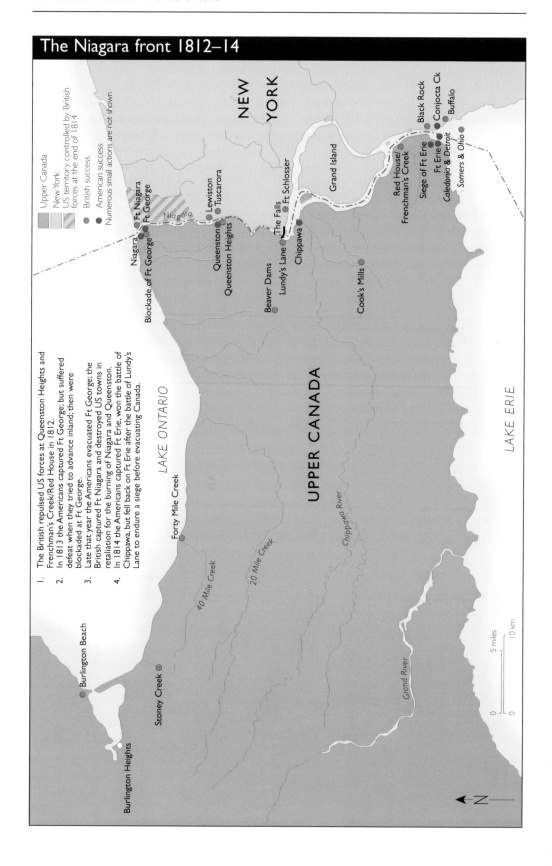

Upper Canada
New York
US territory controlled by British forces at the end of 1814
British success
American success
Numerous small actions are not shown

1. The British repulsed US forces at Queenston Heights and Frenchman's Creek/Red House in 1812.
2. In 1813 the Americans captured Ft George; but suffered defeat when they tried to advance inland; then were blockaded at Ft George.
3. Late that year the Americans evacuated Ft George; the British captured Ft Niagara and destroyed US towns in retaliation for the burning of Niagara and Queenston.
4. In 1814 the Americans captured Ft Erie, won the battle of Chippawa, but fell back on Ft Erie after the battle of Lundy's Lane to endure a siege before evacuating Canada.

NEW YORK

Ft Niagara
Ft George
Niagara
Blockade of Ft George
Lewiston
Tuscarora
Queenston
Queenston Heights
Niagara
Beaver Dams
Lundy's Lane
The Falls
Ft Schlosser
Chippawa
Grand Island
Cook's Mills
Red House/
Frenchman's Creek
Black Rock
Conjocta Ck
Buffalo
Siege of Ft Erie
Ft Erie
Caledonia & Detroit
Somers & Ohio

LAKE ONTARIO

UPPER CANADA

LAKE ERIE

Burlington Beach
Stoney Creek
Forty Mile Creek
40 Mile Creek
20 Mile Creek
Chippawa River
Grand River
Burlington Heights

N

0   5 miles
0   10 km

ABOVE Oliver Perry's victory on Lake Erie captured the imagination of Americans, with the result that artists and engravers created many images of the battle. This particular post-war print is typical of the battle scenes created in the 19th century. (National Archives of Canada)

BELOW A contemporary print of the 1813 battle of Moraviantown. (National Archives of Canada)

British infantry, 1813. On active service, the grenadier on the left normally wore a shako, like the soldier beside him, and both probably wore grey overalls instead of white breeches. Note the belt around the waist of one man, to keep his equipment from moving around – a non-regulation feature representative of the alterations soldiers made for comfort and efficiency. (National Army Museum)

Following this victory, a new commanding officer in Upper Canada, Major-General Francis de Rottenburg, advanced closer to Fort George to constrict the American foothold in the province further. He did not have enough men to retake the post, so he intended to blockade the Americans inside the fort until cold weather brought the campaigning season to an end. (The size of the forces fluctuated during the blockade, but generally the British were outnumbered, at roughly 2–3,000 against 4–5,000 Americans.) De Rottenburg's task was made easier by orders sent from Washington, in light of the recent defeats, telling General Dearborn to avoid action unless necessary and to work on much-needed training. At the same time, in one of his last acts before leaving the Canadian front in disgrace, Dearborn recruited Iroquois warriors from reservations in New York to help address his light infantry deficiency, and what success the Americans did enjoy afterward in pushing back British and native pickets in front of Fort George was largely a result of their efforts. Through the summer that followed, fairly large sorties and raids occurred from time to time, in addition to the almost daily low-level harassment of the American position.

During part of the blockade, the RN's Lake Ontario squadron cruised the mouth of the Niagara River and the south shore of Lake Ontario to intercept supplies and destroy American depots. In general, the naval war on Lake Ontario was a kind of see-saw affair, in which both sides took advantage of small opportunities but avoided a major battle because the consequences of defeat would be devastating for whichever side lost control of the lake. However, there were some encounters. A more important one occurred in early August, when the squadrons tried to catch each other at a disadvantage as part of the operations focused on Fort George. However, the Americans backed off when the British captured two schooners and two others sank in a sudden squall in an engagement known as the Burlington Races.

As the summer wore on, the British found it increasingly difficult to maintain their blockade because of supply problems and widespread sickness in the hot, humid weather. By early October, with General Vincent back in command, they withdrew to comfortable quarters at Burlington Heights, thinking that it was too late in the year for the Americans to pose much of a threat. Yet the invaders showed some energy by making a demonstration toward Burlington, only pulling back when they realized how well entrenched the British were; instead they contented themselves with burning barrack buildings closer to Fort George.

Later, the Americans were no longer in a position to take an aggressive stance on the Niagara Peninsula because they withdrew the majority of troops to participate in a two-pronged offensive against Montreal. One army marched north from Lake Champlain, while the other journeyed down the St Lawrence in 300 small boats (and made a

daring night-run past the British batteries at Prescott). While the British had concentrated a significant portion of their Canadian garrison to protect Montreal, the city lacked good fortifications, and because of its location at the junction of the Ottawa and St Lawrence rivers, its capture would isolate Upper Canada completely. This offensive – the largest American operation of the war, with over 11,000 soldiers – represented a most dangerous threat to the survival of Upper Canada.

One of the American forces, commanded by Major-General Wade Hampton, crossed the border south of Montreal, but on 16 October, at Châteauguay, 3,564 of his soldiers suffered defeat at the hands of a mere 339 well-positioned defenders, consisting mainly of Canadians and natives under Lieutenant-Colonel Charles de Salaberry. Then, on 11 November, the other American thrust, led by Major-General James Wilkinson, came to an inglorious end when 1,169 men under Lieutenant-Colonel Joseph Morrison defeated 3,050 invaders in the open fields of Crysler's Farm, along the banks of the St Lawrence. Hampton and Wilkinson lost all their fighting spirit in the aftermath of these disasters and ordered their armies into winter quarters. Thus ended the gravest threat to Canada posed by the Americans in the war.

Despite their failures in the York-Niagara and Montreal campaigns of 1813, the Americans did enjoy military success in south-western Upper Canada. After the Frenchtown disaster in January, they built Fort Meigs, south of Lake Erie, as a depot and jumping off point to recapture Michigan and invade Upper Canada. Henry Procter and Tecumseh besieged the fort in late April and early May, but could not take it (although losses among the US defenders were very high compared with those on the British side). The British and natives were also repulsed at another post in the region, Fort Stephenson, in one of the small number of instances during the war when they outnumbered their adversaries; and a second attempt to capture Fort Meigs in late July also failed. The result was that the British, and the western tribesmen who followed Tecumseh, retired to Canada and the initiative passed to the Americans.

On 10 September, the American and British squadrons on Lake Erie met for their long-anticipated duel at Put-in-Bay. The British had six vessels, while the Americans had nine better prepared craft, a testimony to their ability to move men and material more efficiently than the British. (American communications routes were much shorter and lay behind the front lines, unlike those of their opponents, which extended all the way through the contested Great Lakes and across the ocean.) Despite the disparities between the squadrons, the battle was a close-fought and bloody affair, but in the end, as the American commander Oliver Hazard Perry famously recorded: 'We have met the enemy and they are ours: two ships, two brigs, one schooner, and one sloop.'

With this defeat, Procter's already tenuous link to the east was cut. Therefore, he destroyed the military works at Detroit and Amherstburg and retreated east toward Burlington, despite outraged protests from Tecumseh and other native leaders who wanted to stand and fight. Meanwhile, Perry ferried an American army across the lake and, with 3,500 men, including 250 American-allied warriors from the Ohio country, under the command of Major-General William Henry Harrison, the Americans pursued Procter. They caught the British and their allies at Moraviantown and defeated some 1,000 men on 5 October. Among those slain was Tecumseh, and with his death and the recent defeats, the native dream of an independent homeland effectively ended. In the weeks that followed, the majority of aboriginal survivors either went home and made peace with the Americans or limped east to seek shelter behind the British lines in Burlington.

The western victories were significant for the Americans and brought their only campaign success on the northern front during the conflict, giving them control of part of Upper Canada and all of Lake Erie.

With their triumph at Moraviantown, the road lay open to strike the Six Nations of the Grand River. These people, hearing stories of atrocities committed by Americans against natives, fled to join the many white settlers and aboriginal refugees from the west in camps behind the British post on Burlington Heights. Even there they did not feel safe, worrying that their redcoated allies would retreat to York, or even to Kingston, because General Harrison stood poised to use the Grand River to get behind Burlington Heights and cut them off.

The British did not leave, partly because they worried that this might cause the natives to go over to the Americans and turn upon the settlers. Fortunately for them, Harrison was satisfied with his achievements on the Thames and chose not to consolidate with a strike eastward. Instead, he retired to Amherstburg, dismissed most of his volunteers, and sent the bulk of his regular force to join the army being formed for the ill-fated Montreal campaign.

There was one more outbreak of fighting along the Canadian border before the close of 1813. With the movement of US troops east to attack Montreal, and the expiration of many militiamen's terms of service, the American garrison at Fort George dropped to less than 600 men by early December. At that point, and with the passing of Harrison's threat to Burlington, the British resolved to recapture the post; their opponents, suffering steady harassment, decided to consolidate their forces on their own side of the border. Before withdrawing, the American commander, Brigadier-General John McClure, turned the people of the town of Niagara out of their houses on a frigid December day and burned down their homes, ostensibly to prevent the British from quartering their troops there over the winter and to improve Fort Niagara's defensibility. The next day, American artillery at Lewiston destroyed part of the village of Queenston by firing red-hot shot (heated canon balls) to set its buildings on fire. The new British commander in Upper Canada, Lieutenant-General Gordon

Drummond, arrived on the peninsula soon afterward, determined to avenge the destruction of these settlements.

Drummond's men crossed the Niagara River and made a surprise night assault on the sleeping garrison of Fort Niagara on 19 December. After a short, sharp fight, the fort fell. The British seized vast quantities of supplies, and killed, wounded, or captured over 400 Americans, losing only 11 of their own. Drummond then cleared the Americans out of the region completely: over the next few days, the settlements along the New York side of the river fell to the torch and the Americans and their native allies suffered a series of small defeats. Once he had captured Buffalo (and destroyed four vessels of the US Lake Erie squadron wintering there), Drummond thought he might continue westward, make a surprise attack on the rest of the American Lake Erie squadron, destroy it, and perhaps even retake Detroit. However, a January thaw melted the ice on the rivers he needed for a quick strike, so Drummond abandoned the idea and retired to the Canadian side of the river, maintaining a garrison on American territory only at Fort Niagara, which the British retained until the return of peace, in 1815.

The United States emerged from the second year of the war in a better position than they had had in 1812. With a number of victories behind them, they had also regained most of the lost territory in the west, occupied a small part of south-western Upper Canada, and seemed to have killed off the possibility of an aboriginal homeland being created at their expense in the Old Northwest. However, their main objective – the conquest of at least all of Upper Canada – had not been accomplished. The British, Canadians, and natives had performed well, despite the odds against them. This had bought the colony another year's grace, but the question now was what would happen with the coming of spring.

1814

Across the Atlantic, the military events of 1812 and 1813 had improved Britain's position in Europe and presented the possibility that far more resources could be applied to the American war in 1814 than had previously been available. In 1812, Napoleon invaded Russia, but rather than conquering the country, endured a disastrous rout in the brutal northern winter. The French emperor suffered additional defeats in 1813 and 1814; then, in March 1814, British and allied armies marched into Paris. Bonaparte abdicated in April, whereupon Britain dispatched significant numbers of reinforcements across the Atlantic.

As the 1814 campaigning season approached with the end of the cold weather, the Americans knew they had to take advantage of the few months that lay ahead before fresh British troops reached Canada. They recognized that the conquest of all the British provinces was no longer viable, but they hoped to secure a good bargaining position in peace negotiations and, if possible, annex Upper Canada.

Logically, their 1814 strategy should have concentrated on the early capture of Kingston or Montreal, with the aim of cutting off the upper province; yet once again they chose to direct their efforts in the west, in part because the battles of Lake Erie and Moraviantown had given them dominance there, a position they enhanced by reoccupying Buffalo after Gordon Drummond abandoned it during the winter.

At the same time, the US government decided not to concentrate its strength on the northern border against one target, but chose to divide it and make two thrusts. One army was to cross the Niagara River from Buffalo, to roll up the Niagara Peninsula, and continue as far east as possible, ideally seizing all of Upper Canada. Hopefully, Britain would relinquish the province in a treaty; at the very least, this would give the Americans something to bargain with if the British were to occupy New England or other parts of the Atlantic region. The second thrust was to sail north from Detroit to retake Mackinac, which had been lost in 1812. The number of men involved in the latter expedition was small, but it was

enough to deprive the commanding officer on the Niagara front of a force that might very well have tipped the balance toward the Americans.

Before these plans could be put into effect, there were a number of confrontations along the Canadian border as the opposing sides tried to achieve advantages in preparation for the upcoming campaigns. In February, the British raided American communities along the St Lawrence River to take supplies. In March, an American army marched against Montreal, but withdrew when it could not dislodge a small force at Lacolle. In May, the British captured Oswego, but another attempt that month to seize naval supplies at Sandy Creek resulted in defeat, and a planned attack on the US Navy base at Sackett's Harbour had to be cancelled for lack of men.

The American expedition against Mackinac called for the recapture of the post and the destruction of enemy military and fur trade operations in the north. The objectives were to regain their lost fort, knock the northern tribes out of the war, and cut the flow of supplies to the native peoples on the Mississippi, who had been fighting the United States despite the defeat of their aboriginal compatriots in Tecumseh's alliance. (See Black Hawk's War, page 66.) Earlier, the Americans had expected that their successes in south-western Upper Canada would have cut the supply line to the west. However, the British had overcome the loss of Lake Erie by sending goods to Mackinac from Montreal, both via the traditional fur trade route that extended up the Ottawa River and along other waterways to Lake Huron, and by moving material west through Kingston to York, then north along a road and water route to Georgian Bay and points to the west.

About 1,000 regulars, militia, and sailors on five vessels of the US Lake Erie squadron, under the command of Lieutenant-Colonel George Croghan of the army and Captain

The amphibious assault on Oswego in 1814, from an 1817 print. (National Maritime Museum)

Arthur Sinclair of the navy, sailed north in July 1814. On their way, they captured two small commercial vessels and burned British fur trade posts. They landed on Mackinac Island on 4 August, planning to advance against the fort. Its commandant, Lieutenant-Colonel Robert McDouall, marched out with 140 soldiers and perhaps as many as 300 militiamen and native warriors and drove the Americans off the island. Defeated, the American commanders sent two vessels south with their casualties and took the other three to Georgian Bay, where they destroyed a fur trade schooner, the *Nancy*, which a small Royal Navy detachment had been operating (although the crew of the *Nancy* got away). Then, one of the three American vessels sailed back to Lake Erie, while the schooners *Tigress* and *Scorpion* headed west to blockade Mackinac. The crew of the *Nancy* set out for Mackinac

in two bateaux and a canoe, accompanied by some natives and fur traders, slipped past the blockade, and obtained permission to try to seize the US schooners. Reinforced with four boats and 50 soldiers, they surprised and captured the *Tigress* in fierce hand-to-hand fighting on 3 September. Three days later, they sailed their prize up to the unsuspecting *Scorpion*, opened fire, then boarded and captured the second vessel. Thus in small-scale fighting, the British kept control over the crucial northern regions as the first snows of the winter of 1814/15 began to blow, and retained the ability to supply their allies in the Mississippi country.

The main American offensive into Canada in 1814 came from Buffalo, with a force that was far better trained and led than any the United States had deployed in the war up to that point. Two years of frustration had led to the replacement of poor quality and incompetent senior officers with better men, and the army as a whole had benefited tremendously from weeks of rigorous training in anticipation of the campaign. On the morning of 3 July, Major-General Jacob Brown led 5,000 soldiers and 600 warriors across the Niagara River against Fort Erie. The 170-man garrison only put up token resistance and then capitulated. When the British commander on the Niagara front, Major-General Phineas Riall, heard about the invasion – but not about the fall of the fort – he rushed south to Chippawa to repel Brown. He also sent some of his native allies and light troops further south to watch American movements and harass any attempt to move north.

On 4 July, one of Brown's brigades, commanded by Brigadier-General Winfield Scott, advanced north with the objective of seizing the bridge across the Chippawa River; Riall's skirmishers harassed their enemy, destroyed the bridge and some nearby buildings that might have provided cover for the Americans, then retired to the north bank of the Chippawa. Scott, faced with the loss of the bridge and a British battery opposite, pulled back and camped for the night along the south bank of Street's Creek.

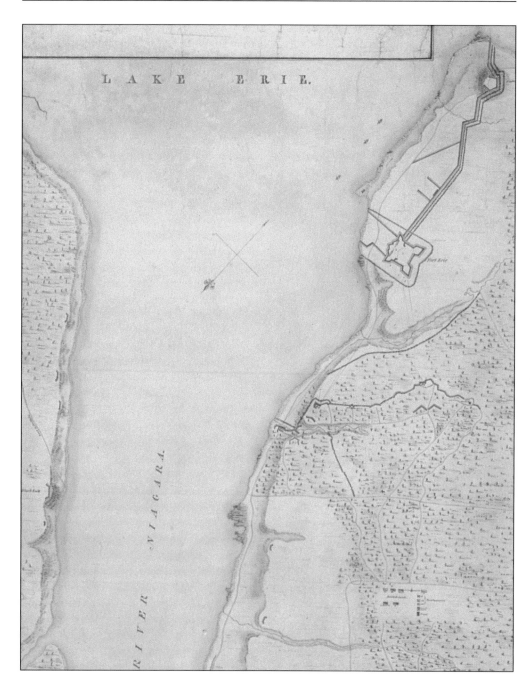

The blockade of Fort Erie, 1814, from a contemporary map. The Americans captured the post in July, and then extended it to accommodate their forces with a long earth wall between the original post and the hill at the top of the map, in time to withstand the British blockade of August–September. The earth 'traverses' in the fort were designed to reduce the devastation of a bombardment. The British lines can be see south of the fort in the forest. (National Archives of Canada)

There the American right flank anchored on the Niagara River, while their left rested 1,400 paces across a field on the edge of a forest. During the night and the next day, the other two brigades in the army arrived in the camp. Riall underestimated the size of the force opposing him, in part because he did not realize that Fort Erie had capitulated, so he assumed that part of Brown's army was investing the place, and in part because some of the American troops arrived in their camp after his patrols had performed their reconnaissance. On 5 July, with about 2,000 men, he decided to attack a force he believed to be a similar size, when in fact the Americans numbered 3,500.

Riall sent his light infantry, Canadian militia, and native allies through the woods to attack the American left; he organized the rest of his regulars to advance across the open plain beside the Niagara River, but without the Americans realizing what he planned to do because the topography hid his crossing of the Chippawa. General Brown, unaware of Riall's movements, already had decided to put an end to some minor harassment he had been suffering from bands of warriors in the forest, and he sent one of his brigades, consisting of regulars, volunteers, and native allies, into the bush to clear out the skirmishers. In the ensuing melee, the brigade inflicted heavy casualties upon the warriors but was repelled when it came up against the light force that had been deployed as part of the larger attack. From the sound of the heavy fire in the forest, Brown assumed that he was probably about to be attacked in force, and he deployed to meet the soon-to-become-visible British troops advancing across the plain. Jacob Brown and Phineas Riall clashed in a classic linear battle. The combined fire of the American artillery and musketry halted the British. A stationary, close-range firefight ensued for the next 20 minutes, then Riall acknowledged defeat, and ordered a retreat. The total number of killed, wounded, captured, and missing may have been as high as 600 on the British side and 350 on the American.

After the battle, both armies returned to their former positions: the British on the north side of the Chippawa River, the Americans on the south side of Street's Creek. Riall then fell back to the mouth of the Niagara River on 8 July, where the British were well entrenched, occupying Forts George and Niagara, as well as a new work,

Fort Mississauga, then under construction. Brown marched to Queenston, where he established a camp, probed the British works to the north, and awaited the arrival of the US Lake Ontario squadron to push his adversaries out of the peninsula completely. Afterward, he hoped to use the ships to move his army against York and Kingston. However, while he waited, he had to be cautious because the British not only had troops in his front at the three forts, but also had men at Burlington Heights and the mouth of Forty Mile Creek who might try to swing behind his rear.

Despite pre-arranged plans, Commodore Isaac Chauncey did not sail his squadron to Brown's assistance, but instead sent a variety of excuses to account for his inaction, even declaring that the navy had a higher calling than that of merely supporting the army! Without Chauncey, and facing losses in men because of sickness, while the British began to receive reinforcements from Europe, Brown decided to retire south to Chippawa. The British marched against the Americans, and the two armies met at dusk on 25 July at Lundy's Lane, not far from Niagara Falls. There 2,800 Americans fought 3,500 men opposite them to a bloody standstill in the confusion of the dark, with the opposing lines pouring devastating volleys into each other from as little as 15 paces apart. The next day, the Americans pulled back, not stopping until they reached Fort Erie. The British, badly bloodied, could not pursue them, which gave Brown time to enlarge and strengthen Fort Erie to house his entire force. At the same time, the US squadron finally arrived, which prevented the British from advancing south because of the threat it posed in their rear and because it stopped supplies being sent from Kingston.

Lieutenant-General Gordon Drummond, who had resumed command on the Niagara Peninsula, moved against Fort Erie early in August and put it under blockade. Unlike Francis de Rottenburg before Fort George in 1813, he intended to retake the post rather than just keep the Americans holed up inside. This proved to be a poor decision because Brown's force was still strong by comparison and because the Americans were able to ferry supplies and reinforcements to the fort from Buffalo with little difficulty (because a British attempt against the town, initiated from Fort Niagara, had been repulsed). Drummond launched an ill-fated assault against Fort Erie on the night of 14 August. It was meant to be a surprise, but the Americans were waiting, and the attack cost Drummond 905 killed, wounded, prisoners, and missing, to only 84 on the American side. The British, frustrated and facing supply problems, sickness, and bad weather, decided to abandon the blockade. While they were preparing to leave, the Americans sortied from the fort on 17 September, spiked three of Drummond's six siege guns, and destroyed ammunition, at a cost of 511 killed and wounded to 606 British killed, wounded, and captured. Drummond retired toward the end of September.

Meanwhile, an American raid along the Lake Erie shoreline by 1,500 men under Duncan McArthur, designed to help Brown in Fort Erie, faltered when it came up against British and Iroquois resistance at the Grand River. Nevertheless, the raiders destroyed mills, farms, and supplies that Drummond had hoped would meet some of his army's needs over the coming winter.

In October, the Americans marched north from Fort Erie in one final attempt to achieve a significant territorial gain. However, after British troops bloodied their advanced detachments at Cook's Mill, word reached the Americans that control of Lake Ontario had fallen decisively to the British, not in a dramatic battle, but by the launch in September of the enormous 104-gun warship HMS St Lawrence. The now powerful RN squadron put the USN under blockade at Sackett's Harbour shortly afterward. With the loss of the lake, the Americans returned to Fort Erie. On 5 November, they blew it up and retired to Buffalo. The 1814 American Mackinac and Niagara campaigns had came to a failed end. Despite most people's

predictions in 1812, with the exception of the small portion of south-western Upper Canada lost in 1813, Canada had survived the third year of the war.

The saltwater war 1812–15

Shortly before declaring war, the American government had deployed warships on the Atlantic Ocean to guard merchantmen on their return home, seize British commercial vessels, and hunt down Royal Navy warships. It was at that early point that the Americans had chased the *Belvidera* to Halifax and this had led the British squadron to sail forth in response. On 16 July, the British sighted and captured the American brig *Nautilus* without a fight. Two days later, they came into contact with the USS *Constitution* and set off in pursuit, but the frigate escaped after a dramatic three-day chase. On 13 August, the American frigate *Essex* overwhelmed the smaller Royal Navy sloop *Alert* in a short engagement off the Grand Banks of Newfoundland. These first encounters defined the fundamental character of high seas confrontations between the two navies for the rest of the war: in most situations, larger and better-armed ships defeated opponents in combat, captured them without a fight, or lost them in a chase.

Occasionally the two navies met on essentially equal terms. The most famous of these incidents occurred in June 1813, when the USS *Chesapeake* sailed out of Boston to meet HMS *Shannon*. The *Shannon* had a smaller crew, but her captain had devoted years to developing his men's gunnery skills. The *Chesapeake* was a better-built frigate, but the crew included a large number of newcomers, some experienced, some not. In 15 minutes of horror, culminating in hand-to-hand fighting as a boarding party descended on the *Chesapeake*, 146 Americans and 83 Britons fell dead or wounded. The US ship surrendered, to spend the rest of her days in the Royal Navy.

The most famous warship in the conflict was the USS *Constitution*. After she had made

The USS *Constitution*, or 'Old Ironsides', from a *c*.1813–15 print. In 1831, Commodore William Bainbridge, who was wounded twice during the frigate's battle with HMS *Java*, reflected on his service on this famous American vessel: 'The ship! Never has she failed us! Never has her crew failed in showing their allegiance and belief in the country they served, or the honor they felt, in belonging to the ship that sheltered them, and on whose decks they fought, where many gave their lives. To have commanded the Constitution is a signal honor; to have been one of her crew, in no matter how humble a capacity, is an equal one. Her name is an inspiration.' (National Maritime Museum)

the dramatic escape from a British squadron mentioned above, she defeated the frigates *Guerrière* and *Java* in August and December 1812 respectively, and inflicted so much damage that both British ships had to be sunk – an unusual event in naval warfare of the time. Although blockaded in port for most of 1813 and 1814, the *Constitution* managed to escape for one cruise in early 1814 and captured a schooner, HMS *Pictou*; then, in February 1815, she met two smaller British warships, the corvette *Cyane* and the

sloop *Levant*, defeating both in a single action, and managed to get the *Cyane* back to the United States after being chased by a squadron of Royal Navy warships.

An important aspect of the naval conflict was the effort made by the British and American governments to use their warships against merchantmen. The British, in particular, also organized convoys to diminish threats to their commercial vessels. One well-known instance of commerce raiding occurred in the summer of 1813, when the USN brig *Argus* ventured into the home waters of the United Kingdom, where merchant vessels were vulnerable because convoys typically broke up near the end of their journeys and made for their various ports of call, and because the RN's strength was deployed to blockade enemies rather than guard the British Isles. Thus the *Argus* took 19 merchantmen in three weeks, until she was captured by HMS *Pelican* in an engagement on 14 August. In another, similar, incident, the USS *Essex* wreaked

The ocean war between the USN and the RN 1812–15

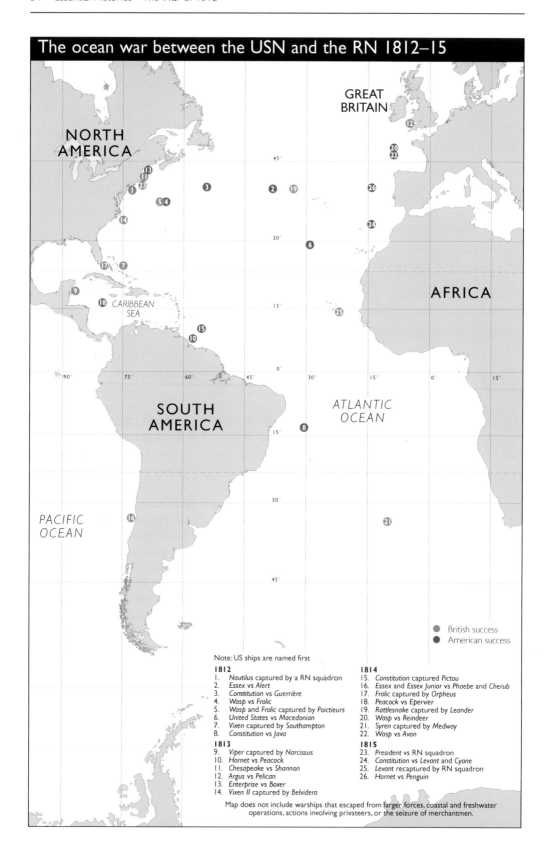

Note: US ships are named first

1812
1. *Nautilus* captured by a RN squadron
2. *Essex* vs *Alert*
3. *Constitution* vs *Guerrière*
4. *Wasp* vs *Frolic*
5. *Wasp* and *Frolic* captured by *Poictieurs*
6. *United States* vs *Macedonian*
7. *Vixen* captured by *Southampton*
8. *Constitution* vs *Java*

1813
9. *Viper* captured by *Narcissus*
10. *Hornet* vs *Peacock*
11. *Chesapeake* vs *Shannon*
12. *Argus* vs *Pelican*
13. *Enterprise* vs *Boxer*
14. *Vixen II* captured by *Belvidera*

1814
15. *Constitution* captured *Pictou*
16. *Essex* and *Essex Junior* vs *Phoebe* and *Cherub*
17. *Frolic* captured by *Orpheus*
18. *Peacock* vs *Epervier*
19. *Rattlesnake* captured by *Leander*
20. *Wasp* vs *Reindeer*
21. *Syren* captured by *Medway*
22. *Wasp* vs *Avon*

1815
23. *President* vs RN squadron
24. *Constitution* vs *Levant* and *Cyane*
25. *Levant* recaptured by RN squadron
26. *Hornet* vs *Penguin*

Map does not include warships that escaped from larger forces, coastal and freshwater
operations, actions involving privateers, or the seizure of merchantmen.

● British success
● American success

havoc on the British South Pacific whaling industry when she captured about half of the ships engaged in the business. In this war against commercial shipping, the USN seized 165 British vessels (and a few troop transports), while the Royal Navy captured 1,400 American merchant vessels and privateers. The RN took some of the privateers into its own service, although it also lost a handful of small schooners and tiny dispatch vessels to larger enemy privateers.

Both Great Britain and the United States licensed privateers to seize enemy ships for profit in a kind of legalized piracy. Some of these privately owned vessels were fast-sailing, heavily crewed craft that preyed upon slow, lightly manned merchantmen. Others were regular ships that would attempt to pick up enemy vessels if opportunities arose during their normal round of business. Privateering was a perilous business: of 526 known American privateers, 148 were captured and others were lost to British action, but only 207 ever took a prize. British privateers, mainly from the maritime provinces of North America, scooped up several hundred prizes, especially among coastal trading craft. At the same time, privateers from the United States captured 1,344 merchantmen from the richer pickings of the British Empire. However, of the vessels taken by American privateers and warships, at least 750 were either recaptured by the British, handed back by neutral powers, or lost at sea, often being burned by their captors once valuable goods had been removed because there was little chance of getting the ships home in the face of RN patrols. Other captured ships had to be used as 'cartels' to return prisoners, and many vessels captured by American privateers were ransomed back to their owners.

The event that had the greatest impact on the ocean war was the Royal Navy's blockade of the American coast, which began informally in 1812 with the modest resources available in the western Atlantic at that time. As more warships took up station off American ports – from roughly 20 in 1812 to 135 at the end of the conflict –

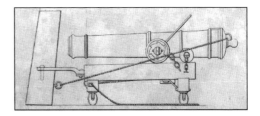

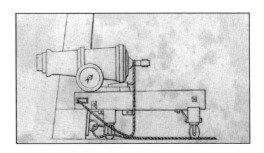

Both navies used guns (top) and carronades (below), shown here in a period print, on experimental carriages. Guns had more range than carronades of the same caliber, but carronades needed less space, smaller crews, and less gunpowder. (Ann Ronan Picture Library)

the RN cut off more and more ports from the outside world. In February 1813, the blockade covered the Atlantic coast between the Delaware and Chesapeake bays (where public sentiment had supported the war more than in other coastal regions). However, New England was exempted, because the British hoped to increase dissension between the north-eastern states that opposed hostilities and the rest of America, and because the British army fighting Napoleon in Spain and Portugal needed American grain to survive, which New Englanders happily supplied in American ships licensed and protected by the British. In March 1813, the Royal Navy expanded the blockade to include Savannah, Port Royal, Charleston, and New York, then extended it again by mid-November to the entire coast south of Narragansett Bay. In May 1814, with Napoleon defeated in Europe and the end of the British army's Iberian supply problems, the RN blockaded New England.

One consequence of the blockade was that the USN could not get its warships out to sea with ease. For example, the super

The *Grand Turk* of Salem, Massachusetts (right), a purpose-built, 14-gun privateer took about 30 prizes, yet the heavily outgunned British packet *Hinchinbrook* (left) beat off an attack in May 1814, as represented in this print from 1819. (National Maritime Museum)

frigates *United States* and *Macedonian*, accompanied by a smaller warship, set sail to prey upon British West Indian shipping in 1813 but had to flee back to port when a Royal Navy squadron intercepted them. Both frigates then sat out the rest of the war, as did the largest and most dangerous ships the USN built during the conflict – six new super frigates and four even larger ships-of-the-line. Provisioned and maintained from bases in Newfoundland, Nova Scotia, Bermuda, and the West Indies (and often replenished by profit-seeking American civilians in coastal waters), the blockading ships not only locked up much of the US saltwater navy in port, but also dissuaded many privateers from leaving home. Despite the tightening noose, some vessels did manage to escape the blockade to fight the RN or raid British commerce.

Most importantly, the blockade devastated America's international trade. Between 1811, the last full year of peace, and 1814, the value of American exports and imports fell from $114 million to $20 million and the customs revenues needed to finance the war

Attacking the United States 1813–15

Beginning in February 1813, British naval and army commanders used modest reinforcements from Europe to launch destructive raids against the Chesapeake region, close to Washington. For the most part, they met only ineffectual resistance as they destroyed military, naval, maritime, and industrial targets and captured a large number of sailing vessels. They also burned or took property when the locals opened fire or otherwise resisted them or did not offer the British ransoms against the seizure or destruction of their possessions (although those who remained quietly at home generally were left in peace and were paid for supplies requisitioned to support these British operations). Raids took place elsewhere along the Atlantic coast too, particularly in areas where the population undertook hostile acts against the blockaders. Among the several dozen operations, most of which were successful, six boats from a blockading naval force rowed up the Connecticut River in April 1814 to torch seven privateers, 12 large merchantmen, and 10 coastal vessels, while Stonington, Connecticut, endured the miseries of a naval bombardment a month later because the British thought the town was sheltering men who planned to sail booby-trapped vessels up to Royal Navy warships in order to blow them up.

With the fall of Napoleon in 1814, the British expanded their operations against the American Atlantic coast, undertaking larger initiatives as well as raids. In August, they landed 4,000 men near Washington and on 22 August, Royal Marines and sailors struck at the American gunboat flotilla on the Patuxent River; over the following day the Americans lost a privateer, 17 gunboats, and 13 merchant schooners, either captured, or destroyed by retreating US forces. On 24 August, part of the British force, numbering 2,600, easily defeated 6,000 militia, sailors, and regulars at Bladensburg in a very short battle, leaving

fell from $13 million to $6 million (despite a doubling of the rates). At the same time, the cost of trade within the United States increased dramatically as people abandoned the efficient coastal lanes for slow overland routes. By 1814, only one out of every 12 merchant ships in the United States even dared to leave port, dramatically exemplifying the economic impact of the war on the republic's economy. For the British, in contrast, international trade grew in the same period, from £91 million in 1811 to £152 million in 1814, despite American actions that brought death, destruction, and heartache to ship owners, seamen, and their families.

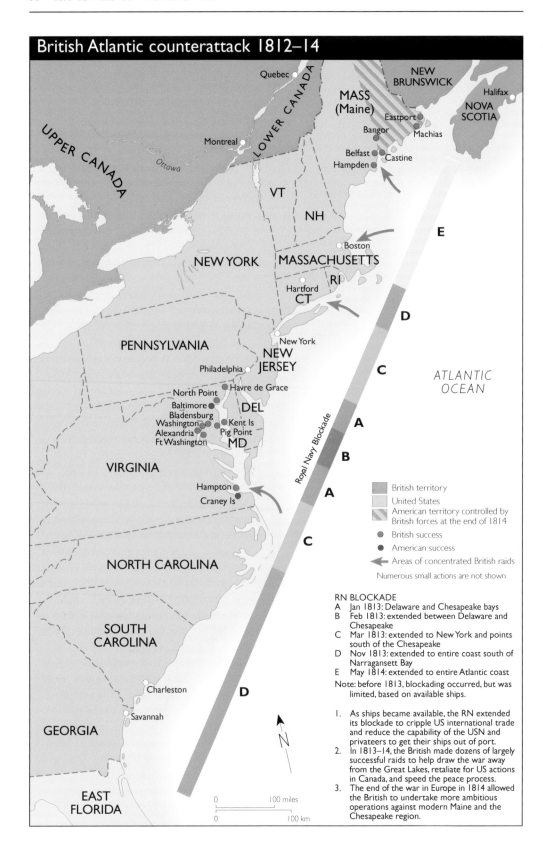

British Atlantic counterattack 1812–14

Quebec
LOWER CANADA
UPPER CANADA
Ottawa
Montreal

NEW BRUNSWICK
Halifax
MASS (Maine)
NOVA SCOTIA
Eastport
Bangor
Machias
Belfast
Castine
Hampden

VT
NH
E
Boston
NEW YORK
MASSACHUSETTS
RI
Hartford
CT

PENNSYLVANIA
New York
NEW JERSEY
Philadelphia
D

C
ATLANTIC OCEAN

North Point
Havre de Grace
Baltimore
Bladensburg
DEL
Washington
Kent Is
Alexandria
Pig Point
Ft Washington
MD

VIRGINIA

Royal Navy Blockade

A
B
A
C

Hampton
Craney Is

NORTH CAROLINA

SOUTH CAROLINA

Charleston

Savannah

GEORGIA

EAST FLORIDA

D

British territory
United States
American territory controlled by British forces at the end of 1814
● British success
● American success
← Areas of concentrated British raids
Numerous small actions are not shown

RN BLOCKADE
A Jan 1813: Delaware and Chesapeake bays
B Feb 1813: extended between Delaware and Chesapeake
C Mar 1813: extended to New York and points south of the Chesapeake
D Nov 1813: extended to entire coast south of Narragansett Bay
E May 1814: extended to entire Atlantic coast
Note: before 1813, blockading occurred, but was limited, based on available ships.

1. As ships became available, the RN extended its blockade to cripple US international trade and reduce the capability of the USN and privateers to get their ships out of port.
2. In 1813–14, the British made dozens of largely successful raids to help draw the war away from the Great Lakes, retaliate for US actions in Canada, and speed the peace process.
3. The end of the war in Europe in 1814 allowed the British to undertake more ambitious operations against modern Maine and the Chesapeake region.

0   100 miles
0   100 km

This contemporary print presents a fanciful composite of the 1814 attack on Washington. The destruction of the US gunboat flotilla is in the lower foreground, the battle of Bladensburg is in the upper right, and the burning of the public buildings and navy yard are on the left. (Library of Congress)

an American officer, Joseph Sterett, to remark: 'We were outflanked and defeated in as short a time as such an operation could well be performed.' Among those in retreat was James Madison.

Meanwhile the president's wife, Dolley (or Dolly), saved as much as she could from the presidential mansion, including one of the nation's iconographic artifacts, a portrait of George Washington attributed to Gilbert Stuart. As the British continued their march on the capital, the commandant of the Washington navy yard burned its extensive facilities as well as a frigate and a sloop, while other people blew up a nearby fort at Greenleaf's Point. The victorious redcoats entered the capital unopposed and set fire to the White House, Capitol, Treasury, and War Office, as well as various military facilities.

They also took large quantities of munitions and weapons before starting back to their ships the next day. Meanwhile, other British soldiers and sailors were moving upriver against Fort Washington. Expecting a fight, they were surprised when the Americans blew up the fort and retreated. The British then took Alexandria on 27/28 August and seized 21 prize vessels as well as other goods. As the squadron withdrew, the Americans set up shore batteries to destroy the British ships, but the raiders experienced little trouble taking them on and making it back to sea by early September.

The British then moved against Baltimore, home of much of the privateering fleet and hence a city that deserved, in the minds of many officers, to be either destroyed or compelled to pay an enormous tribute in order to be spared. The navy sailed to the mouth of the Patapsco River on 11 September to land troops, before continuing on to attack Fort McHenry. The army came ashore the next day and marched against the city. On the way, an advanced

ABOVE The White House, after being burned by British forces, from a contemporary print. When opposition politicians in London condemned the torching of public buildings in Washington, Prime Minister Lord Liverpool offered the justification that American forces on the Canadian front had 'displayed a ferocity which would have disgraced the most barbarous nations. In one instance, a town [Niagara] was, in the middle of December, committed by them to the flames, and the inhabitants then driven … into the open country amidst all the severities of a Canadian winter. On another occasion, when the town of York, the capital of Upper Canada, was occupied by the Americans they burnt the public buildings, and took possession of the property of the governor as such. It was a retaliation for this excess that the public buildings at Washington were destroyed.' (Library of Congress)

BELOW The 1814 battle of Plattsburg, from a contemporary print. (National Maritime Museum)

guard fell into an ambush, and although it drove the Americans away, the commanding officer, Major-General Robert Ross, the victor of Bladensburg, was mortally wounded in the action. The redcoats continued, ran into a large force blocking the way to the city, but pushed it aside at the battle of North Point. On 13 September, the British advanced further, but halted when they came up against the well entrenched Americans, who outnumbered them by three to one. Believing that their only hope lay in a surprise night attack, the British decided to wait until midnight before striking. On the American side, some pessimists burned the ropewalks that supplied the city's ships and schooners along with a new USN frigate. The Royal Navy began a 25-hour bombardment of Fort McHenry and another battery with artillery and rockets on 13 September from such evocatively named bomb and rocket vessels as *Volcano*, *Aetna*, *Meteor*, and *Devastation*. However, the fleet could not get close enough to its targets, in large part because the people of Baltimore had sunk 24 merchant vessels to block the way. At the same time, a squadron of American gunboats threatened its rear. The

fleet commander, Vice-Admiral Sir Alexander Cochrane, decided to pull back, and he sent word to those on shore that a withdrawal probably would be wise because the odds were too great. The officers on the scene called off the planned landward assault and marched back to the ships on 14 September. Despite losing the actions outside of the city, the Americans had good reason to be jubilant. Fort McHenry had held out and Baltimore had been saved.

On the northern frontier, the governor of British North America, Sir George Prevost, invaded New York with reinforcements from Europe. He marched south late in the summer of 1814 with 10,000 men, intending to capture the border community of Plattsburgh on Lake Champlain and secure Lower Canada's vulnerable underbelly. However, the United States Navy had built up a formidable squadron on the lake. Prevost knew this would have to be destroyed before he could move since he did not think it would be safe to operate with such a force in his rear. He ordered the British squadron on the lake into action on 11 September, although its commanding officer did not think it ready but hoped that support from Prevost directed against American shore batteries would give him victory. The British naval force – a frigate, a brig, two sloops, and 15 gunboats with 90 guns – met the US squadron carrying 88 guns spread between two sloops, a brig, a schooner, and 10 gunboats and galleys (with additional support from the shore batteries). About an hour after the lake battle began, Prevost ordered his army to advance on Plattsburgh itself, but he left the batteries alone. About half an hour later, the British squadron was defeated, and its commander, George Downie, lay dead under an overturned 24-pounder. Prevost, unwilling to move with the American squadron threatening his back, cancelled the attack and withdrew to Canada, to the outrage of the officers under his command and the delight of the Americans, who rewarded their commander, Thomas Macdonough, with praise and a promotion.

Two regiments of black troops, including the 5th West India Regiment pictured in this 1815 image, served in the New Orleans campaign. Other blacks, such as in Upper Canada, fought in regular, volunteer, and militia units. Many free blacks within the US helped to defend their country, but some slaves, such as several hundred from the Chesapeake region, joined the British. Most blacks, with little reason to trust either side, avoided participation in the war. (National Army Museum)

The British, however, enjoyed success elsewhere in the north, when troops from Nova Scotia occupied the Maine district of Massachusetts. They first took Moose Island, on 11 July 1814, then Castine, on 1 September. Two days later, they attacked Hampden and dispersed a militia and naval force. During that action, the Americans burned a corvette to prevent her capture. On 5 September the British marched into Bangor and took a large number of merchant vessels. They then seized Machias. The occupiers treated the local population, which capitulated on 13 September, with respect, and reopened trade with the outside world.

Toward the end of the war, far to the south, the British attacked the American Gulf coast. Until that time, the south had been a backwater in the Anglo-American crisis, but the United States had been engaged in two parallel conflicts in the region. In 1812, Spain, a country recently allied to Britain, ruled East and West Florida but was unable to pay much attention to these colonies because it was busy trying to expel the French army from its own motherland. In October 1810, President Madison proclaimed the annexation of West Florida and sent troops to occupy much of the colony; then, in 1813, he took more land. In 1812, filibusters from Georgia invaded East Florida but enjoyed only minimal success. (Later, in 1819, the United States purchased Florida from Spain.) North of Florida, the aboriginal people who made up the Creek nation tore themselves apart in a civil war in 1813–14. The conflict stemmed from deep internal tensions over whether or not to sell land and adapt to white ways; it brought American intervention when traditionalists began to attack the white

settlers. The conflict devastated the Creek population and ended with survivors either fleeing to Spanish territory or signing away half their territory to the United States. During the American conflicts with the Spanish and Creeks, the British made half-hearted efforts to intervene to support their own objectives, but at best they played marginal roles.

In the final year of the fighting, the British hoped to seize the lower portions of

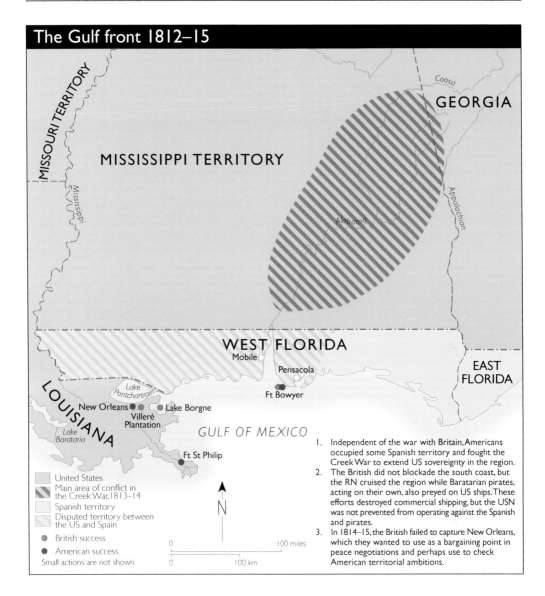

The Gulf front 1812–15

MISSOURI TERRITORY

Coosa

GEORGIA

MISSISSIPPI TERRITORY

Mississippi

Alabama

Appalachian

WEST FLORIDA

Mobile

Pensacola

EAST FLORIDA

Lake Pontchartrain

New Orleans   Lake Borgne

LOUISIANA

Villeré Plantation

Ft Bowyer

Lake Barataria

GULF OF MEXICO

Ft St Philip

United States

Main area of conflict in the Creek War, 1813–14

Spanish territory

Disputed territory between the US and Spain

● British success

● American success

Small actions are not shown

N

0   100 miles
0   100 km

1. Independent of the war with Britain, Americans occupied some Spanish territory and fought the Creek War to extend US sovereignty in the region.
2. The British did not blockade the south coast, but the RN cruised the region while Baratarian pirates, acting on their own, also preyed on US ships. These efforts destroyed commercial shipping, but the USN was not prevented from operating against the Spanish and pirates.
3. In 1814–15, the British failed to capture New Orleans, which they wanted to use as a bargaining point in peace negotiations and perhaps use to check American territorial ambitions.

the Mississippi River to use as a bargaining chip in peace negotiations – or even to affirm Florida's independence from the United States and perhaps create a separate state in the lower Mississippi because the ethnic diversity of the region and the American government's tenuous authority there suggested that the map could be redrawn. The first major British act was to send an inadequately small force on a failed expedition to capture Fort Bowyer at Mobile Point in September 1814, in preparation for a larger assault against New Orleans. The expedition against this main target, however,

had to wait until the blistering summer and hurricane seasons were over. After assembling troops in Bermuda and the West Indies, the British sailed to New Orleans, arriving near their target in December with a force of 7,500 men.

Anticipating the attack, Major-General Andrew Jackson dispatched a flotilla of gunboats to Lake Borgne to guard one of the approaches to New Orleans. Royal Marines in small ships' boats attacked them on 14 December and captured all of the USN vessels. This helped the British land near the city, with assistance from Spanish and

Portuguese fishermen, who held little regard for the American government. However, unusually cold weather, combined with the deep swamps and difficult terrain, made the advance on the city very difficult, created serious supply problems, and contributed to a large number of deaths through illness and exposure. Then, on 23 December, Jackson led a combined naval and land attack against the British in their camp at the Villeré Plantation outside of the city. The redcoats held their own in the confused night action and the Americans pulled back.

This painting, probably from the 1820s, shows small British boats rowing to capture American gunboats on Lake Borgne. Gunboats typically were 40–60 feet (12–18m) long and were armed with one or two 18-, 24-, or 32-pounder guns, firing respectively 8, 11, and 15kg shot. (National Maritime Museum)

Jackson then fortified the approach to New Orleans at the Rodriguez Canal, which he equipped, in part, with artillery, powder, and shot supplied by the local Baratarian pirates who had allied themselves to their erstwhile enemies in the face of the British invasion. Meanwhile, the commander of the British expedition, Major-General Sir Edward Pakenham, ordered the destruction of a gunboat, the *Carolina*, which had participated in the attack on Villeré plantation, with red-hot shot. On 28 December, he performed a reconnaissance in force against Jackson's line, but was forced to withdraw, despite coming close to breaking one of the American flanks. Then, on 1 January 1815, he bombarded the Americans, hoping to silence their guns, but with little effect because the British did not have enough ammunition and because their

An 1815 British map showing their operations against New Orleans that ended in disaster. (National Maritime Museum)

guns became bogged down in the soggy ground. American artillery fire did considerable damage in return. A week later, on 8 January, the British made their famous but notoriously ill-executed frontal assault against Jackson. They carried one of Jackson's batteries at bayonet point, but the main assault collapsed into disaster, and Pakenham fell in the action. The British withdrew, having suffered their worst defeat in the war, and, like the Americans, having fought the battle in ignorance of news that diplomats had agreed to terms of peace on 24 December.

In the short New Orleans campaign, the British suffered 2,450 killed, wounded, missing, and captured, to only 350 losses on the US side. They nevertheless maintained their fighting spirit and later made two more attacks against American posts – one that failed, against Fort St Philip near New Orleans, and one that succeeded, against Fort Bowyer, which capitulated on 11 February and which the British took in preparation for a move against Mobile. The next day, however, word of the peace treaty arrived, and the soldiers and sailors shifted their attention to the task of preparing to go home.

Black Hawk's war

In 1833, the Sauk war chief, Black Hawk, looked back over his life and dictated his memoirs, which were translated into English for publication. There are a few problems with them, such as some obvious interventions by the translator or publisher, along with numerous chronological lapses, but they provide a fascinating first-hand account of one warrior's life around the time of the War of 1812.

Black Hawk was born in 1767 at Saukenuk, the principal tribal town, on the east bank of the Mississippi River. At the age of 15, he took up the ways of the warrior and wounded his first enemy. Shortly afterward, he joined his father in a campaign against the Osages, a tribe that lived to the south-west of his own people, and was 'proud to have an opportunity to prove to

him that I was not an unworthy son, and that I had courage and bravery.' Excited with 'valor and ambition,' Black Hawk 'rushed furiously upon another, smote him to the earth' with his tomahawk, ran his lance through his body, and took his scalp, while his father watched, said nothing, but 'looked pleased.' Upon returning home, he joined the other warriors in his first triumphal scalp dance, then continued fighting to protect his tribe's access to hunting lands from other aboriginal challengers and to avenge the killing or capture of members of his nation.

A new period of challenge began in 1804, when American officials assumed control of the fur trade community of St Louis following the 1803 Louisiana Purchase in which the United States acquired sovereignty over the vast territories on the west side of the Mississippi River from France. Although Sauk territory had fallen within the boundaries of the United States previous to that time, American influence had been minimal. However, in 1804, the newcomers invited four Sauk leaders to St Louis, where they used alcohol to befuddle them into signing a fraudulent treaty, alienating an enormous amount of Sauk (and Fox) land as a condition for restoring peace with the settler population following an outbreak of low-level hostility between natives and the

Black Hawk (from a print done in the wake of the Black Hawk War). He found American and British modes of combat to be deficient, noting in disgust: 'Instead of stealing upon each other and taking every advantage to *kill the enemy and save their own people*, as we do (which with us is considered good policy in a war chief), they march out in open daylight and *fight*, regardless of the number of warriors they may lose! After the battle is over they retire to feast and drink wine as if nothing had happened; after which, they make a *statement in writing* of what they have done – *each party claiming the victory!* and neither giving an account of half the number that have been killed on their own side.' (Peter Newark)

The Upper Mississippi front 1811–15

United States
American territory controlled by British forces at the end of 1814
British or native success
American success
Numerous small actions are not shown

Ft Shelby/McKay
Prairie du Chien
Wisconsin
LAKE MICHIGAN
MICHIGAN TERRITORY
Ft Dearborn
Campbell's Island
Rock Is Rapids
Saukenuk
Rock
MISSOURI TERRITORY
ILLINOIS TERRITORY
Des Moines
Ft Madison
Illinois
Mississippi
Mississinewa
Ell
Tippecanoe
INDIANA TERRITORY
Wabash
Ft Harrison
N
Sink Hole
Missouri
St Louis

1. Low-grade hostilities occurred between whites and natives before the war, which escalated with the US attack on Tippecanoe in 1811, but the scale of violence in 1812–15 remained small compared to other fronts.
2. The Americans tried to assert control over the region north of St Louis, using the Mississippi as their main communications line; however, the natives and British dominated the upper Mississippi.

0 50 miles
0 100 km

newcomers. The Sauks were allowed to remain in the ceded territory until the US sold it to settlers. This treaty, combined with tensions arising from increasing settlement, led Black Hawk and many in his nation to maintain friendly relations with the British in Canada in the hope that the British might help the Sauks to overturn the treaty and secure the independence of their homeland. However, another Sauk group, the peace band, chose the path of neutrality and accommodation, partly because the growing American presence was changing their trade and other relationships, and partly because

its members did not believe they could oppose the United States successfully.

Black Hawk then learned about the efforts by Tecumseh and Tenskwatawa to form their pan-tribal confederacy, remembering ruefully how 'runners came to our village from the *Shawnee Prophet* … with invitations for us to meet him on the Wabash. Accordingly a party went from each village. All of our party returned, among whom came a *Prophet*, who explained to us the bad treatment the different nations of Indians had received from the Americans by giving them a few presents and taking their land from them. I remember well his saying, "If you do not join your friends on the Wabash, the Americans will take this very village from you!" I little thought then that his words would come true! Supposing that he used these arguments merely to encourage us to join him, we agreed that we would not.'

Despite his coolness to the Shawnee brothers, Black Hawk remained hostile to the Americans and rejected the legitimacy of the 1804 treaty. Naturally, he participated in the slowly escalating opposition to the United States, which exploded into war in 1811 at Tippecanoe. Once the Anglo-American war had broken out in 1812, Black Hawk led a war party in an attempt to take Fort Madison near his village, but it failed. In early 1813, he responded to a call by British officials to lead 200 men away from his homeland to the Detroit frontier, where he saw action at Frenchtown and at forts Meigs and Stephenson. When he returned to the Mississippi early in 1814, he learned how the conflict had transpired there during his absence. In many ways, this was a classic frontier struggle with both the natives and settlers organizing small-scale raids against each other and attacking non-combatants. Perhaps the best news from Black Hawk's perspective was the burning and evacuation of Fort Madison by its American garrison in September 1813 following a summer of aboriginal harassment. This 'pleased' him because 'the white people had retired from our country.'

As the 1814 campaigning season opened in the spring, the locus of American strength in the west was St Louis. To the north, the British occupied the fur trade village of Prairie du Chien and used it to encourage and supply native allies along the Mississippi who continued to oppose the Americans (unlike many of the tribesmen of Tecumseh's alliance, who had been knocked out of the war after the battle of Moraviantown). The fighting that ensued repeated the patterns of raids and harassment set earlier, and also saw a more energetic American response to try and subdue the tribes and evict the British.

The Americans sent troops up the Mississippi in fortified gunboats to intimidate the tribes, and, in June, they entered Prairie du Chien without resistance because the small garrison had abandoned the village in the face of their advance. They then built Fort Shelby but surrendered it after a short British siege in July. (The victors renamed the post Fort McKay.)

Black Hawk fought in the 1814 Mississippi campaign, including an engagement at Campbell's Island in July and the battle of the Rock Island Rapids in September. At the latter, he defeated Major Zachary Taylor, the future president, who retreated downriver after the fighting. At the former, high winds drove one of the American vessels aground. Black Hawk declared: 'This boat the Great Spirit gave us!' and led an assault against it. He remembered: 'We approached it cautiously and fired upon the men' who had come ashore from the stricken vessel. Faced with the attack, the Americans 'hurried aboard, but they were unable to push off, being fast aground.' Black Hawk continued: 'We advanced to the river's bank, under cover and commenced firing at the boat. Our balls passed through the plank and did execution, as I could hear them screaming in the boat! I encouraged my braves to continue firing. Several guns were fired from the boat, without effect.' Then he prepared a bow and arrows 'to *throw fire to the sail,* which was lying on the boat; and after two or three attempts succeeded in setting the sail on fire. The boat was soon in flames!' Then one of the other vessels in the flotilla attempted to rescue the stranded soldiers. Black Hawk recalled that it 'swung in close to the boat on fire, and took off all the people except those killed and badly wounded. We could distinctly see them passing from one boat to the other, and fired on them with good aim. *We wounded the war chief in this way!'*

At this point, another American vessel came by and dropped anchor to assist the beleaguered boat, but the anchor did not take hold and the gunboat drifted ashore while the first rescue boat abandoned the fight. With another vulnerable target, Black Hawk's band 'commenced an attack' and 'fired several rounds' but the crew did not shoot back. Thinking his enemy was afraid or had only a few men on board, he ordered his men to rush the stricken craft. 'When we got near, they *fired*, and killed two of our people, being all that we lost in the engagement.' Then: 'Some of their men jumped out and pushed off the boat, and thus got away without losing a man!' This show of bravado impressed Black Hawk, who declared: 'I had a good opinion' of the boat commander because he 'managed so much better than the other,' and in fact Black Hawk noted that it 'would give me pleasure to shake him by the hand.'

Word of the war's end reached the upper Mississippi in May 1815, when an American vessel from St Louis carried the news up to Prairie du Chien. The British invited their aboriginal allies to a council and told them that they had to end their hostilities. An angry and defiant Black Hawk held up a black wampum belt that had been given to him early in the conflict and declared: 'I have fought the Big Knives, and will continue to fight them till they are off our lands. Till then my father, your Red Children can not be happy.' He then led his followers against the Americans, with the most notable action of 1815 being a skirmish known as the 'battle' of the Sink Hole. Other Sauks, however, signed a treaty with the United States in 1815. A year later, Black Hawk acknowledged the wider peace and he too agreed to stop fighting.

After the war, whites pressured the Sauks to move to the west side of the Mississippi. Black Hawk told the story of one friend that symbolized the tensions of the era, recalling how, on an island in the Rock River, he 'planted his corn; it came up well – but the white man saw it! – he wanted the island, and took his team over, ploughed up the corn, and re-planted it for himself. The old man shed tears; not for himself, but the distress his family would be in if they raised no corn.' In 1831, with Black Hawk's band continuing to oppose removal, troops surrounded Saukenuk, opened fire with artillery, and then moved in. The village, however, was empty; its people had fled across the Mississippi during the previous night. The Americans torched their homes and desecrated their graves, perhaps knowing how important sites associated with the spiritual world were to the Sauks.

A cowed Black Hawk agreed to live in the west, but when the Americans failed to live up to promises to provide food in compensation for the loss of crops at Saukenuk, he and other leaders brought 1,000 or more Sauks, Foxes, and other native men, women, and children home again in April 1832. The so-called 'Black Hawk War' ensued, but it amounted to little more than a brutal series of tragedies for a short time and culminated in the butchering of the majority of Black Hawk's followers when they tried to swim back across the Mississippi River under fire. Black Hawk gave himself up to the Americans, who toured him through the eastern United States to demonstrate their power and thereby prevent further troubles. It was upon his return to the Mississippi that he dictated his memoirs.

Black Hawk lived out his remaining days quietly in the shadow of the sadness of all that his people had lost, passing away in 1838. Shortly afterward, a white man broke into his grave and stole his remains. They were put on display in a museum, and then were lost in a fire.

Mississippi region natives in 1814. Note the military-style 'chief's coat' on one man, presented by British authorities to aboriginal leaders. He also wears 'chief's medals' around his neck as tokens of alliance. Note as well the black man beside him. Tribes in 1812 often adopted outsiders – native, white, and black – into their ranks. (National Archives of Canada)

Propaganda and protest

Propaganda

Both sides used propaganda to advance their cause, boost morale among their people, and win approval on the international stage. One example of this was the reluctance of the United States to speak openly about expansion as a reason for war, preferring instead to condemn Britain and the tribes for affronting American rights on the Atlantic and in the Old Northwest. Likewise, the British played down maritime tensions and concentrated on issues related to defending their colonies and assisting the natives in protecting their homelands. Troops from both armies committed crimes against civilians (although on a comparatively small scale), but each side made a point of expressing indignity when their enemy was the perpetrator, even to the point of gross exaggeration. Bald-faced lies were another element of this propaganda war. After the battle of York in 1813, for example, Americans read broadsides proclaiming that their soldiers had dispersed 1,000 warriors in the action, when in fact native combatants opposing them numbered only 40–60 men.

Much of the propaganda war focused on the natives. US newspapers regularly condemned such 'Indian atrocities' as scalping and the desecration of the dead; yet the reality was that both the natives and the Americans scalped and committed indignities upon the other. In 1812, for instance, US Brigadier-General Alexander Smyth offered $40 bounties for native scalps, while a year later, another American officer, George McFeeley, saw a Kentuckian who 'had two Indian scalps that he had taken at Frenchtown' and who 'fleshed them with his knife, salted them, and set them in hoops in true Indian style.' American propaganda also roundly condemned native enemies for killing prisoners after the battle of Frenchtown on the Raisin River, which generated the war cry, 'Remember the Raisin!' to motivate their troops in the Old Northwest. However, their newspapers (and subsequent historians) remained silent about American acts of brutality, such as the murder, scalping, and disfigurement of a captured British soldier and Canadian militiaman a few months later, in which the militiaman had not been killed before being butchered. For their part, the tribespeople expressed bewilderment at the dissonance between words and deeds, such as occurred in 1813, when British officers reprimanded some warriors for mutilating an American corpse. An Ottawa chief, Black Bird, replied with the complaint that their enemy had disinterred aboriginal dead and chopped up the bodies, then declared: 'If the Big Knives when they kill people of our color leave them without hacking them to pieces, we will follow their example.'

Protest

Many people opposed their leaders' decisions in the War of 1812. Among natives, individuals generally were free to stand aside from a community decision to engage in hostilities or at least determine the extent to which they would support the general consensus, even to the point of being able to desert in the face of enemy fire without

RIGHT Scalp, c.1812, consisting of skin and hair stretched to a wooden hoop with sinew. Many natives believed that spiritual power was concentrated in the scalp and that enemy scalps could be 'adopted' into a family grieving the loss of a loved one in order to strengthen its spiritual power and to serve as proof that the lost person had been avenged. (City of Toronto Museums and Heritage Services)

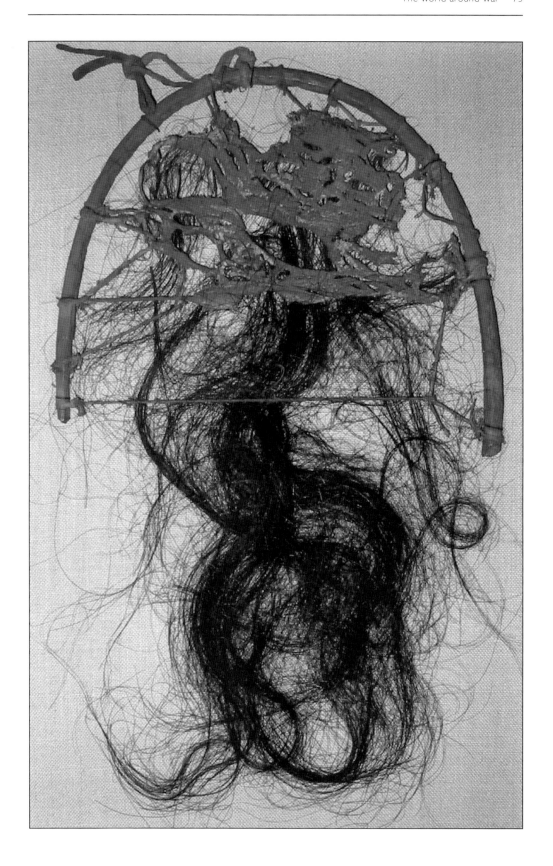

*Bring me the Scalps
and the King our master
will reward you.—*

*Reward for
Sixteen
Scalps*

Cartoonists on both sides produced crude propaganda to sell to patriotic consumers. This 1812 American image denounces the British for purchasing scalps, something that the British did not do. In fact, they offered bounties to their native allies for prisoners to discourage the killing of captured enemies. (Library of Congress)

serious repercussions. Within the white world, militia service was not voluntary: men were obliged to turn out when called, although the regular armies on both sides were composed of volunteers. Yet American, British, and Canadian society allowed people considerable freedom to frustrate the wishes of officialdom or speak in opposition to their government. Thus, for example, in 1812, the legislative assembly of Upper Canada could reject Isaac Brock's request to suspend some civil liberties in order to allow the army to defend the province more effectively. In New England, the Revd Elijah Parish could comfortably denounce James Madison for going to war against Britain, which he saw as the bulwark against Napoleonic absolutism, with the words: 'If we engage in this war, then we take the side with the despot; we enlist

under his fatal banner ... and must share in his approaching destruction.'

The ability of the state to exert its authority was also limited enough that many who violated laws, such as militiamen who went home when they became dissatisfied, usually suffered no serious repercussions. Treason – helping the enemy – of course, could bring the death penalty, but even then there were far fewer prosecutions than there were incidents. Often, assisting the enemy was overlooked when territory was occupied, as happened when the British army marched

on Washington in 1814 and people sold livestock, offered to guide the way to the capital, and provided intelligence to the redcoats. Afterward, however, individuals might find themselves ostracized by their friends and acquaintances.

On the British side, the most dramatic event that involved cases of aiding the enemy was the 'Bloody Assize' of May and June 1814. Held in Ancaster, on the Niagara Peninsula, a court tried 19 residents of Upper Canada who had been captured while serving with the Americans. Charged with high treason, four were acquitted, one admitted his guilt, and 14 were found guilty on the evidence brought against them. Before imposing the death sentence, the judges held back the executions for a month to give the men the opportunity to supplicate royal mercy. After the time had passed, eight died at the end of a hangman's noose. The other seven were reprieved pending further consideration (three based on the recommendations of the judges involved and four as a result of petitions from the condemned men's friends and families). Two of these seven escaped custody and fled to the United States, three died during an outbreak of disease in jail, and the remaining three received pardons on condition that they leave the British Empire for the rest of their lives.

For Americans, the most memorable story of potentially traitorous activity was that of the Hartford Convention of December and January 1814/15. Held in the Connecticut state capital, it arose from New England's frustrations with the war. Washington's defensive efforts in the region were inadequate, and the states felt they needed to keep control of their own militia forces despite federal government attempts to direct their operations. Madison's tax increases were proving worrisome, and the British blockade and raids, as well as the occupation of part of the region itself, created enormous consternation. As the convention met, some New England newspapers called for secession from the American Union and the signing of a separate peace with Britain. The federal government was so worried about the convention that it sent troops to Hartford in case there was an attempt to take New England out of the republic. However, most of the delegates were far more moderate than the press, and, despite the misunderstandings of the Madison administration and subsequent popular

memory, it was not a seditious enterprise. Its final report did not pose a challenge to the republic, being instead a plea for change to restore New England's declining powers within the Union. As one politician, Josiah Quincy, noted when asked what he thought its outcome would be, the worst consequence he could come up with was 'A great pamphlet!'

John Strachan's war

John Strachan, born to a modest Scottish family in 1778, crossed the Atlantic in 1799 to find work as a tutor in Upper Canada. Toward the end of his contract, he sought holy orders in the Church of England and was ordained deacon in 1803 and priest in 1804. He served the church at Cornwall on the St Lawrence River, married a wealthy young widow, Ann Wood McGill, and established the best school in the backwoods colony, for which he received an honorary doctorate of divinity from the University of Aberdeen. In 1812, he moved to the provincial capital of York to take up duties as rector of the parish, headmaster of the York District Grammar School, and chaplain to both the garrison and the provincial parliament.

His own sense of loyalty was both conservative and steadfast, so the content of his first major war sermon to the colony's parliament was no surprise. In a long and impressive address, he tried to resolve the problems of being both a soldier and a Christian, largely by affirming that the Christian was a moral and restrained combatant when fighting for a just cause. He entered political controversy by supporting the suspension of some civil liberties because of the crisis, which most of the politicians in his congregation did not want to do, and he addressed other issues that troubled the people of Upper Canada as they faced the imminent prospect of foreign invasion.

Shortly afterward, Strachan was overjoyed to learn about the surrender of Detroit and the capture of the Northwestern American army, leading him to declare: 'The brilliant victory … has been of infinite service in confirming the wavering & adding spirit to the loyal.' This was a real concern to him because the British cause had seemed to be almost hopeless at the outbreak and because so many people in the province were, as he

Silhouettes of John Strachan and his wife, Ann, in 1807. (Toronto Reference Library)

wrote, 'recently from the States and by no means acquainted with the obligations which they contract when they come to live under this government' and so 'a signal advantage gained over the enemy was therefore necessary to keep them to their duty.'

Strachan's war efforts were not confined to pulpit pronouncements. He encouraged the young women of York's leading families to embroider flags for the local militia regiment and he organized a subscription to provide shoes and clothing for militiamen serving on the Niagara Peninsula. He even helped to alleviate problems created by a wartime shortage of coinage and small-denomination paper money by organizing the York Association, where merchants could deposit bullion and army bills (the *de facto* currency of the province) in return for small denomination notes to facilitate commerce, and then used the interest the association earned for poor relief. Then, inspired by a suggestion from a young woman in his congregation, Elizabeth Selby, he founded the Loyal and Patriotic Society of Upper Canada at the end of 1812. It raised a substantial £21,500 in British North America, the West Indies, and the United Kingdom to relieve distressed militiamen and their families, subsidize the cost of bread because wartime inflation caused hardships for the poor, and engage in other charitable acts during the conflict. After the war, the society used its surplus to establish a general hospital in York.

As garrison chaplain, Strachan not only welcomed soldiers and their families to his church, but he held additional services for them (such as occurred when there were too many people to fit into his small clapboard house of worship), and carried out marriages, churchings, baptisms, and burials. During the conflict, the army established military hospitals in York, and Strachan visited the sick and wounded twice each week. During weekday visits he usually spoke privately to the patients, asked after their health, and 'dropped something concerning their spiritual welfare.' He also gave out religious tracts, Bibles, and prayer books, but never had enough to keep up with the demand for these publications (which says something about the views and literacy of common British soldiers that clash with the general image of them as 'the scum of the earth'). On Sunday visits he also read prayers and delivered 15–20 minute homilies. Since ambulatory patients followed him through the hospitals to hear his sermons, he felt that he had to preach something different in each ward, with the result that he sometimes gave five distinct addresses during a single visit, which he found fatiguing. As casualties mounted and as space to care for them became scarce, Strachan agreed to turn his church over to the army in 1814 to be used

as a hospital. Faced with ministering to large numbers of patients, a great many of whom Strachan wrote were 'sadly mangled' from their battlefield injuries, and having to bury as many as six or eight souls a day during particularly grim periods, he lamented: 'I wish that those who are so ready stirring up wars would traverse the field of battle after an engagement or visit the hospitals next day and they would receive a lesson that might be very beneficial to them in future.'

Strachan's most dramatic contributions during the war occurred at the time of the battle and occupation of York, in late April and early May 1813. During the fighting, he evacuated wounded men from one of the

batteries until it fell to the Americans and the British regulars retreated from the capital. Once the battle was over, he joined senior militia officers to negotiate a capitulation with the Americans. They surrendered those soldiers remaining in the community, consisting mainly of wounded men and the militia, and turned over government supplies to the invaders. In return, the US commanders agreed to respect private property, allow the civil government to function without hindrance, and let surgeons and others attend to the British wounded.

Despite these terms, American troops, including some officers, broke into homes, molested and robbed the townspeople, and pillaged Strachan's church. They also locked up the British and Canadian wounded to languish without food, water, or medical attention for two days. On the day after the battle, an outraged Strachan stormed up to the enemy leaders, Major-General Henry Dearborn and Commodore Isaac Chauncey, to demand that they abide by the conditions of the capitulation. At first these officers tried to brush the priest aside, but he stood his ground and eventually they agreed to post sentries in the town, release the

The barracks at York, where John Strachan served as garrison chaplain, as depicted in 1804. (National Archives of Canada)

wounded into his care, and feed the prisoners. Over the next two days he moved the injured to private homes, procured food, clothing, medicines, and dressings for them, and even provided what treatments he could. Looting continued, however, and at one point, Strachan rescued one of his parishioners from a gang of Americans who were about to shoot her while robbing her home. With these ongoing violations of the terms of surrender, Strachan called a meeting of the town magistrates to produce a list of grievances to give to the American commanders. Dearborn 'promised everything,' as Strachan recorded, and increased the town guard, but robberies continued and in another violation of the agreement, US forces torched the governor's home and the parliament buildings before leaving after their short occupation.

The war years proved to be profoundly traumatic for the Strachan family. In 1812, one of Ann and John's children died, plunging them into a deep grief. A few months later, John received a letter telling him that his mother had passed away in Scotland. After the battle of York, he sent Ann and their children to Cornwall because he thought they would be safer there, but the decision brought personal horror when American soldiers moved through the town and a gang of them robbed, assaulted, and probably raped Ann, who was pregnant at the time, and who was left in such a state of emotional and physical collapse that her family and friends despaired of her life. Thankfully, she recovered and gave birth to a baby girl in early 1814, but then, just after the return of peace, the Strachans' home in York was gutted by fire.

Word of the end of hostilities and the survival of Upper Canada within the British Empire reached York in February 1815. In early April, the people of the town attended a special service of thanksgiving at which John Strachan preached the sermon. He looked to the postwar period with hope: 'Since the return of Peace, a great change is observable among our inhabitants, many are desirous of religious instruction who used to be cold and indifferent.'

In looking back over the war with America, as well as Britain's larger conflict with France, Strachan searched for divine purpose in the conflicts that had engulfed his world and which he said had resulted in Britain's triumph over its enemies, something that few had expected in 1812, when the United States 'with horrid joy' grasped at expansion at the very moment when Britain was mired in the European crisis. Despite Britain's own failings, he believed that King George's subjects at home and in the colonies had 'abundant cause to give thanks to Almighty God for the successful issue of the contest; that we are a free and happy people; have never bowed to a foreign yoke; and have preserved in all its vigour our most excellent constitution.'

Strachan's wartime service brought him public recognition that led him into the corridors of power in the backwoods province, where he tried to impose a High Tory ideology that had been shaped by his wartime experiences. His objective was to create an ordered and deferential society on the frontier, based on the twin pillars of an established Church of England and the British constitution. However, the colony was too diverse for this in religious terms to be acceptable, and the times were too liberal and democratic for his old-fashioned notions of civil society to develop. Gradually, even officials in York and London turned their backs on him, and by the 1830s he had become a political anachronism.

Fortunately for Strachan, his church began to be reinvigorated by ideas that emanated from the Oxford Movement, which suggested a new and independent role for Anglicanism, less tied to the state but more attached to its older traditions and roles. After his consecration as bishop of the newly created diocese of Toronto in 1839, he worked tirelessly for his church until his death in 1867 – the same year that some of the British North American colonies came together to form a new nation within the British Empire, the Dominion of Canada.

The peace of Christmas Eve

The Treaty of Ghent

During the winter of 1814/15, both sides assumed that fighting would resume in the spring. They strengthened their forts and fleets and otherwise made their plans. However, these efforts became pointless as word arrived that the war had ended. Much of eastern North America had heard the news by February 1815, although some isolated posts, such as Prairie du Chien, had to wait until the spring to learn of the return of peace. After three years of hostility, people moved quickly to return their lives to normal. For example, the RN commander at Kingston, Sir James Lucas Yeo, accepted an invitation from his old rival, Commodore Isaac Chauncey, to visit Sackett's Harbour with his fellow officers, who, in their hurry to get back to England, took the fastest route home, via New York City. Sadly, the good news took longer to reach some of the more distant parts of the world, with the result that far away in the Indian Ocean on 30 June 1815, the USS *Peacock* fired upon the small East India Company brig *Nautilus*, killing and wounding 14 people, despite the fact that officers from the British vessel had come aboard the *Peacock* with news that the war was over.

Efforts to end the conflict had begun almost as soon as it had broken out, when the American *chargé d'affairs* in London suggested an armistice in return for a renunciation of impressment (the Orders-in-Council having been revoked before the outbreak), but the British were unwilling to concede on that issue. Shortly afterward, when the British captured Detroit and news of the repeal of the Orders reached North America, Sir George Prevost arranged an armistice with the American commander on the northern front, Henry Dearborn, to

enable the United States government to reconsider its plans. However, the administration of James Madison decided to continue the war, having set its sights on the conquest of Canada. In March 1813, Russia offered to mediate a peace, but the British government rejected the opportunity because it might compromise British interests in Europe. However, in January 1814, both powers agreed to negotiate with each other directly and settled on the then-Dutch city of Ghent as the meeting place, having rejected their initial choice, Gothenburg in Sweden, as too isolated. Diplomats from the two nations first met in August 1814.

Both sides used the changing see-saw in fortunes across the Atlantic to push for as many concessions as possible, although the fundamental difference between the two powers was that the primary British objective was to maintain the 1812 status quo by retaining Canada and asserting Britain's maritime rights, except, if possible, to force the United States to accept the creation of a native homeland in the Old Northwest. The Madison administration essentially wanted to alter the status quo dramatically, by annexing Canada, changing Britain's naval policies and practices, and eliminating aboriginal resistance in the west. At times, such as when the news of the fall of Washington reached Ghent but not the withdrawal of British forces from Baltimore, British diplomats naturally tried to get more from the Americans – such as land cessions and a demilitarization of the Great Lakes – to improve Canada's security. The Americans made forlorn attempts to win Upper Canada through diplomacy while their army was failing to do so militarily.

Both sides wanted the war to end if national dignity could be maintained. The main British objective of keeping Canada had been met as of 1814, and they feared it might be endangered if the war were to continue; at the same time, the fragile peace established in Europe showed enough signs of disintegration that the troops recently sent to North America were needed back on the Continent. Furthermore, British taxpayers cried out for relief, having borne the costs of fighting wars and subsidizing allies for 20 years. The Americans realized that their own objectives in going to war could not be achieved, and thought the best they could probably get was the preservation of the status quo that they had been fighting so hard to upset. Conquest was proving impossible, and in fact the British controlled more US territory than the Americans occupied in Canada. The Orders-in-Council had been revoked before the outbreak of hostilities, and while the British would not relent on impressment and other policies, the end of the European war promised to render concern for at least some of these issues academic. At the same time, the United States faced bankruptcy, recruitment for the army had fallen below the rate at which men were being lost, and federal officials did not appreciate just how weak was the secessionist movement in New England. Thus, American diplomats dropped their demands for a resolution of Anglo-American maritime problems and for restitution for damages done during the blockade and coastal raids, along with their claim for compensation for, or the return of, slaves who had sought freedom with the British, and for the cession of Canada. Both parties also agreed to make peace with the native peoples and restore to them the rights they had enjoyed in 1811 – a move that had far more impact on the United States than it did on Great Britain because of the aboriginal situation in the Old Northwest. All captured territory, except for some islands in Passamaquoddy Bay, off Maine, that the British had seized, were to be returned to their 1812 owners, and other issues, such as conducting a scientific survey of the Canadian-American border to determine an

exact boundary line, were left to be settled in the future. The Americans also agreed to assist the British in suppressing the slave trade. On 24 December 1814, the diplomats signed the peace treaty, with most of its articles being based on the principle of *status quo ante bellum*, and then joined together to celebrate the coming of Christmas in Ghent cathedral.

On 26 December, London business interests had learned enough to shift their investments in anticipation of renewed trade with the United States, and on 27 December the Prince Regent (the future George IV) ratified the document. Across the Atlantic, the US Senate unanimously ratified the treaty on 17 February 1815, and at 11.00 p.m. that night the war officially ended with an exchange of ratifications. In Britain, the government learned about the events in Washington on 13 March, and with the coming of spring, both sides withdrew their forces from the territories of their former enemy and began to send prisoners-of-war home. Within the aboriginal world, negotiations took place through 1815 and 1816 to end the fighting between the tribes and the respective white powers they had fought against, also to bring hostilities to a close among the tribes that had fought against each other.

Perceptions of victory

As word filtered across the Atlantic that peace had returned, most Americans, like their British counterparts who had heard the news earlier, sighed with relief as the associated burdens and uncertainties lifted and they could look to a future with greater promise. Most Americans seemed to forget why their country had gone to war, the failure of their soldiers, sailors, and diplomats to achieve their objectives, and instead embraced the memories of successes at Plattsburgh, Baltimore, and especially New Orleans to bolster an interpretation of the peace that affirmed the independence and dignity of their country, going so far as to proclaim that they had won a 'second war of independence.' Some pronounced their enthusiasm for the outcome with a surprising degree of hyperbole: Congressman George Troup declared the Treaty of Ghent 'the glorious termination of the most glorious war ever waged by any people.' For his part, President James Madison told Congress, on 18 February 1815, that the war had been a success.

As time passed, the legends of American victory grew. The famous Democratic-Republican party newspaper *Niles Register*, on 14 September 1816, crowed: '... we did virtually dictate the treaty of Ghent to the British,' ignoring completely that it had been a scramble just to get the status quo of 1812, let alone achieve any war aims, while vague affirmations that Britain had come out of the war with a new-found respect for the United States helped to solidify such views. This attitude has remained dominant in the American public consciousness, as can be seen in today's brochures and web presentations from 1812 historic sites as well as in textbooks and the popular media, and even in much academic writing. Other Americans in 1815 saw things differently. While some thought of the war fundamentally as a draw, many Federalist party supporters who had opposed the Madison administration noted how the government had failed to achieve its goals. These views, less helpful in building national identity and patriotism, have been embraced by far fewer Americans, both then and in subsequent decades.

An assessment of objectives set in 1812 and realized in 1814 points to a British victory, although perhaps one that is not clear in the modern mind, partly because the war occurred in an age when diplomatic negotiations, the preservation of dignity, and compromise marked treaties, rather than the images of unconditional surrender that have come to dominate our consciousness. Furthermore, a successful defensive war has less impact on the popular imagination than a conflict that changes national boundaries. On maritime issues, the British understood that their prewar policies risked conflict with the United States, but they believed that they could not abandon these policies because of the imperative to defeat Napoleon. Yet, as the possibility of hostilities loomed larger, they rescinded the Orders-in-Council to avoid a confrontation before the US declaration, and so the revocation of the Orders had nothing to do with the war itself.

Britain would not, however, negotiate a compromise on impressment or other maritime policies, such as excluding American ships from trade routes it wanted to keep for exclusive British use, and thus the peace treaty was silent on these points and did not challenge British policies or practices. That impressment evaporated as a problem between the two powers was due entirely to Britain's triumph over France and had nothing to do with American actions, and the United Kingdom came out of the war fully prepared to implement any restrictions it wished if future tensions required them. More importantly, Britain defended its North American colonies successfully, and thus the Canadian experiment in building a distinct society was not brought to a violent and premature close through American conquest, but continued, as it does today. This was the most significant outcome of the War of 1812. For Britain, the retention of these colonies (and their subsequent identity as a nation within the Empire) gave it access to North American products outside of the control of the United States, and also contributed to the overall strength of the Empire; it also provided the mother country with absolutely critical support in both 1914 and 1939 when Canada went to war (while the United States stayed out of the great conflicts of the 20th century until 1917 and 1941 respectively).

While the case for a fundamental British victory over the United States is the most logical one that can be made, there were other participants in the conflict whose stories muddy the waters. Although their fights had only the most peripheral links to the war, the contemporary struggles of

DEFENCE OF FORT M'HENRY.

The annexed song was composed under the following circumstances—
A gentleman had left Baltimore, in a flag of truce for the purpose of getting released from the British fleet, a friend of his who had been captured
at Marlborough.—He went as far as the mouth of the Patuxent, and was
not permitted to return lest the intended attack on Baltimore should be
disclosed. He was therefore brought up the Bay to the mouth of the Patapsco, where the flag vessel was kept under the guns of a frigate, and
he was compelled to witness the bombardment of Fort M'Henry, which
the Admiral had boasted that he would carry in a few hours, and
that the city must fall. He watched the flag at the Fort through the
whole day with an anxiety that can be better felt than described, until
the night prevented him from seeing it. In the night he watched the Bomb
Shells, and at early dawn his eye was again greeted by the proudly waving
flag of his country.

TUNE—ANACREON IN HEAVEN.

O ! say can you see by the dawn's early light,
   What so proudly we hailed at the twilight's last gleaming,
Whose broad stripes and bright stars through the perilous fight,
   O'er the ramparts we watch'd, were so gallantly streaming?
And the Rockets' red glare, the Bombs bursting in air,
Gave proof through the night that our Flag was still there;
     O ! say does that star-spangled Banner yet wave,
     O'er the Land of the free, and the home of the brave ?

On the shore dimly seen through the mists of the deep,
   Where the foe's haughty host in dread silence reposes,
What is that which the breeze, o'er the towering steep,
   As it fitfully blows, half conceals, half discloses ?
Now it catches the gleam of the morning's first beam,
In full glory reflected new shines in the stream,
     'Tis the star spangled banner, O ! long may it wave
     O'er the lard of the free and the home of the brave.

And where is that band who so vauntingly swore
   That the havoc of war and the battle's confusion,
A home and a country, shall leave us no more ?
   Their blood has washed out their foul footsteps pollution
No refuge could save the hireling and slave,
From the terror of flight or the gloom of the grave,
     And the star-spangled banner in triumph doth wave,
     O'er the Land of the Free, and the Home of the Brave.

O ! thus be it ever when freemen shall stand,
   Between their lov'd home, and the war's desolation,
Blest with vict'ry and peace, may the Heav'n rescued land,
   Praise the Power that hath made and preserv'd us a nation!
Then conquer we must, when our cause it is just,
And this be our motto—" In God is our Trust ;"
     And the star-spangled Banner in triumph shall wave,
     O'er the Land of the Free, and the Home of the Brave.

The best-known patriotic legacy of the war is *The Star Spangled Banner*. This is the first known printing of the lyrics, probably made right after the bombardment of Fort McHenry. The words are by Francis Scott Key, who set them to the music of a British song, *To Anacreon in Heaven*. In 1889 the USN began using *The Star Spangled Banner* at flag-raising ceremonies, a practice copied by the army. In 1931, Congress made it the US national anthem. (Maryland Historical Society)

Spanish Florida and the Creek nation in resisting US expansion failed. Much more closely related to the war between Great Britain and the United States were the ordeals of natives in the north and west, who divided roughly into Canadian-resident natives, who largely (if conditionally) supported the British, American-resident natives, who allied with the Americans, and those who lived within the borders of the United States but fought against the Americans. This last group was the largest and potentially the most vulnerable. The Treaty of Ghent included an article that stated that all these peoples were to have their territorial and other rights of the prewar period returned. This was far less than the native homeland that the majority of natives of the Old Northwest wanted, but the one campaign the Americans had won on the Canadian front was on the Detroit frontier. This made it difficult to argue for a homeland without a corresponding willingness on the part of the British to continue waging war to achieve that goal. Such a course of action was simply not in the interests of either Britain or Canada, and the natives, as the junior partner in the alliance, like junior partners throughout history, had their interests sacrificed to those of the dominant party. Nevertheless, the article was not insubstantial.

The problem with the treaty, however, was that it did not preclude the United States from working to alienate native lands and reduce aboriginal rights after having restored them to their 1811 status. Ironically, those natives who had fought as allies of the US, such as the Iroquois in New York, received no better treatment from the Americans after 1815 than those who had opposed the United States.

Native people in Canada also suffered, as settlement pressures accelerated the alienation of their lands, although this occurred at a slower pace and without the degree of violence and dislocation that marked the experience of the tribes south of the Canada-US border.

The world's longest undefended border?

The end of the War of 1812 brought permanent peace between Great Britain and the United States, and politicians at cross-boundary events today like to speak of the world's longest undefended border, claiming that it has existed since 1815. The reality is somewhat different. Military planners in 1815 did not know that peace would last, so they prepared for another conflict, and both sides agreed that the reason the Americans had failed to conquer Upper Canada was that they had not severed the St Lawrence supply line by capturing either Kingston or Montreal. Thus, both sides

strengthened fortifications, focusing particular attention on the St Lawrence. The British, for example, built a massive citadel in Kingston in the 1830s and added several Martello towers to the town in the 1840s. Most ambitious of all, they built the Rideau Canal to create an alternative water route to the vulnerable St Lawrence, hoping that in a future war it would allow them to keep supply lines open to the upper province. The Americans improved their forts and built roads to facilitate future invasion attempts. They also worked to cut the ties between the British in Canada and the tribes of the Old Northwest, mainly through removing the natives farther west. In part, these efforts were little more than prudent planning by the British and American governments, rather than serious preparations for conflict, but both powers thought of the other as a potential enemy in the decades that followed.

The British built the Rideau Canal in the 1820s–30s to bypass the St Lawrence River above Montreal in case the Americans should seize control of the waterway in another war. This 1839 image shows the locks and defensive blockhouse on the canal at Merrickville. (National Archives of Canada)

Nevertheless, neither power wanted war, and in general their diplomats tried to ease tensions whenever problems arose. Both countries also wanted to avoid unnecessary expenditure on military preparedness; thus in 1816–17, the British minister to Washington,

Sir Charles Bagot, and the acting US secretary of state, Richard Rush, negotiated a naval disarmament for the northern border. Accepted in 1817, the Rush-Bagot Agreement limited each power to maintaining a small number of armed vessels across the Great Lakes and on Lake Champlain. Most of the 1812-era warships were put into 'ordinary' for future use or were sunk, broken up, or sold to civilians. Yet, in spite of that agreement and general aspirations to avoid hostilities, both sides still eyed each other suspiciously from time to time and, in fact, both violated Rush-Bagot during periods of tension. However, a

After the end of hostilities, both sides secured their warships for future use, as can been seen in this 1815 image of Kingston, Upper Canada. Note the roof over one of the ships and how others have had their masts removed for storage. From left to right, note: Fort Henry, the top of a blockhouse (behind the workers), Navy Bay and its naval dockyard, the town waterfront, and the civilian community. (National Archives of Canada)

breach never occurred, and in 1917, over a century after the end of the War of 1812, the United States joined France, Britain, Canada, and the other colonies of the Empire on the Western Front in the great struggle against Germany and its allies.

Legacies

The War of 1812 was a small conflict compared with the great Napoleonic wars that were its contemporaries and that contributed to its genesis. This has meant that the British largely have forgotten the conflict. In the United States, memories survived, but to a large degree were subsumed by those of a more congenial war, the one with Mexico in 1846–48, in which the United States expanded into Texas, California, and other regions due to a military establishment that had been improved dramatically in light of the experiences of 1812–15. Afterward, the great national crisis of the Civil War shook Americans and eclipsed the conflicts with Britain and Mexico in the public consciousness. In Canada, the War of 1812 was the most acute crisis of the

19th century, and it dominated the popular imagination, resulting in a series of impressive centennial celebrations in 1912–14. Even today, with Britain, Canada, and the United States being firm friends, and with their shared experiences of the wars of the 20th century, Canadians still hold the War of 1812 to be one of the great moments in their country's history.

The Stoney Creek Monument was built by the 'people of Canada' through the efforts of the Women's Wentworth Historical Society and was 'unveiled by electricity' by Queen Mary from Buckingham Palace in 1913 on the centennial of the battle. Part of the monument's text reads: 'Here the tide of invasion was met and turned by the pioneer patriots and soldiers of the King of one hundred years ago. More dearly than their lives they held those principles and traditions of British liberty of which Canada is the inheritor.' (Battlefield House Museum)

Further reading

Primary Sources

Benn, C. (ed) *Warriors: native memoirs from the War of 1812* (Toronto: forthcoming)

Black Hawk, A. LeClair (trans), J. Patterson & D. Jackson (eds) *Life of Black Hawk* [1833] (Urbana, 1990)

Brannan, J. (ed) *Official letters of the military and naval officers of the United States during the war with Great Britain* (Washington, 1823)

Congreve, W., *An elementary treatise on the mounting of naval ordnance* (London, 1811)

Cruikshank, E (ed.), *The documentary history of the campaigns on the Niagara Frontier, 1812–14*, 9 vols (Lundy's Lane, 1902–08)

Duane, W., *American military library* (Philadelphia, 1809)

Dudley, W., (ed.) *The naval War of 1812: a documentary history*, 4 vols (Washington, 1985-)

Gellner, J. (ed), *Recollections of the War of 1812: three eyewitnesses' accounts* (Toronto, 1964)

Graves, D. (ed), *Merry hearts make light days: the War of 1812 journal of Lieutenant John Le Couteur, 104th Foot* (Ottawa, 1993)

Graves, D. (ed), *Soldiers of 1814: American enlisted men's memoirs of the Niagara campaign* (Youngstown, 1996)

Klinck, C. & Talman, J. (eds), *The journal of Major John Norton, 1816* (Toronto, 1970)

Latour, A. G. Smith (ed), *Historical memoir of the war in West Florida and Louisiana in 1814–15, with an atlas* [1816] (Gainesville, 1999)

Malcomson, R. (ed), *Sailors of 1812: memoirs and letters of naval officers on Lake Ontario* (Youngstown, 1997)

Myers, M., *Reminiscences 1780 to 1814: including incidents in the War of 1812–14* (Washington 1900)

Wilson, J., 'A rifleman at Queenston,' *Buffalo Historical Society Publications* 9 (1906)

Wood, W. (ed), *Select British documents of the Canadian War of 1812*, 4 vols (Toronto, 1920–28)

Secondary Sources

Allen, R., *His Majesty's Indian allies: British Indian policy and the defence of Canada, 1774–1815* (Toronto, 1992)

Altoff, G., *Amongst my best men: African-Americans and the War of 1812* (Put-in-Bay, 1996)

Barbuto, R., *Niagara 1814: America invades Canada* (Lawrence, 2000)

Benn, C., *Historic Fort York* (Toronto, 1993)

Benn, C., *The Iroquois in the War of 1812* (Toronto, 1998)

Benn, C., 'A Georgian parish' in W. Cook (ed), *The parish and cathedral of St James'* (Toronto, 1998)

Bowler, R. (ed), *War along the Niagara: essays on the War of 1812 and its legacy* (Youngstown, 1991)

Burt, A., *The United States, Great Britain, and British North America from the Revolution to the establishment of peace after the War of 1812* (New Haven, 1940)

Calloway, C., *Crown and calumet: British-Indian relations, 1783–1815* (Norman, 1987)

Chartrand, R., *Uniforms and equipment of the United States forces in the War of 1812* (Youngstown, 1992)

Chartrand, R. & G. Embleton, *British forces in North America 1793–1815* (London, 1998)

Collins, G., *Guidebook to the historic sites of the War of 1812* (Toronto, 1998)

Cruikshank, E., 'Blockade of Fort George,' *Niagara Historical Society Transactions* 3 (1898)

Everest, A., *The War of 1812 in the Champlain Valley* (Syracuse, 1981)

Fredriksen, J., (comp) *Free trade and sailors' rights: a bibliography of the War of 1812* (Westport, 1985)

Fredriksen, J., (comp) *War of 1812 eyewitness accounts: an annotated bibliography* (Westport, 1997)

Gardiner, R. (ed), *The Naval War of 1812* (London, 1998)

George, C. (ed), *Journal of the War of 1812* (1995-)

Glover, R., *Britain at Bay: defence against Bonaparte 1803–14* (London, 1973)

Graves, D., *Red coats and gray jackets: the battle of Chippawa* (Toronto, 1994)

Graves, D., *Where right and glory lead! The battle of Lundy's Lane, 1814* revised edition (Toronto, 1997)

Graves, D., *Field of glory: the battle of Crysler's Farm 1813* (Toronto, 1999)

Gray, W., *Soldiers of the king: the Upper Canadian militia 1812–1815* (Erin, 1995)

Heidler, D. & J. *Old Hickory's war: Andrew Jackson and the quest for empire* (Mechanicsburg, 1996)

Heidler, D. & J, (eds) *Encyclopedia of the War of 1812* (Santa Barbara, 1997)

Hickey, D., 'The Monroe-Pinkney treaty of 1806: A Reappraisal,' *William and Mary Quarterly* 44 (1987)

Hickey, D., *The War of 1812: a forgotten conflict* (Urbana, 1989)

Hickey, D., 'The War of 1812: still a forgotten conflict?' *Journal of Military History* 65 (2001)

Hitsman, J., *Safeguarding Canada, 1763–1871* (Toronto, 1968)

Hitsman, J., (revised D. Graves) *The incredible War of 1812* (Toronto, 1999)

Horsman, R., *Expansion and American Indian policy 1783–1812* (Norman, 1992)

Kert, F., *Prize and prejudice: privateering and naval prize in Atlantic Canada in the War of 1812* (St Johns, 1997)

Lord, Walter *The dawn's early light* (New York, 1972)

Mahan, A., *The influence of sea power upon the War of 1812*, 2 vols (Boston, 1905)

Malcomson, R., *Lords of the lakes: the naval war on Lake Ontario 1812–1814* (Annapolis, 1998)

Malcomson, R., *Warships of the Great Lakes, 1754–1834* (London, 2001)

Martin, T. A., *most fortunate ship: a narrative history of Old Ironsides*, revised edition (Annapolis, 1997)

Morris, J., *Sword of the border: Major General Jacob Brown 1775–1828* (Kent, 2000)

Owsley, F., *Struggle for the Gulf borderlands: the Creek War and the battle of New Orleans 1812–1815* (Gainesville, 1981)

Owsley, F., *Filibusters and expansionists: Jeffersonian Manifest Destiny, 1800–1821* (Tuscaloosa, 1997)

Petrie, D., *The prize game: lawful looting on the high seas in the days of fighting sail* (Annapolis, 1999)

Pfeiffer, S & Williamson R (eds) *Snake Hill: an investigation of a military cemetery from the War of 1812* (Toronto, 1991)

Pratt, J., *Expansionists of 1812* (Gloucester, Mass, 1957)

Quimby, R., *The US Army in the War of 1812: an operational and command study*, 2 vols (East Lansing, 1997)

Roosevelt, T., *Naval War of 1812* (New York, 1882)

Skaggs, D. & G. A. Altoff, *A signal victory: the Lake Erie campaign 1812–1813* (Annapolis, 1997)

Skelton, W., 'High army leadership in the era of the War of 1812: the making and remaking of the officer corps,' *William and Mary Quarterly* 51 (1994)

Stagg, J., *Mr Madison's war: politics, diplomacy and warfare in the early American republic 1783–1830* (Princeton, 1983)

Stagg, J., 'Enlisted men in the United States Army, 1812–1815,' *William and Mary Quarterly* 43 (1986)

Stagg, J., 'Between Black Rock and a hard place: Peter B. Porter's plan for an American invasion of Canada in 1812,' *Journal of the Early Republic* 19 (1999)

Stagg, J., 'Soldiers in peace and war: comparative perspectives on the recruitment of the United States Army, 1802–1815,' *William and Mary Quarterly* 57 (2000)

Stanley, G *The War of 1812: land operations* (Ottawa, 1983)

Sugden, J., *Tecumseh: a life* (New York, 1997)

Sutherland, S., *His Majesty's gentlemen: a directory of British regular army officers of the War of 1812* (Toronto, 2000)

Tucker, S., *Arming the fleet: US Navy ordnance in the muzzle-loading era* (Annapolis, 1989)

Tucker, S., *The Jeffersonian gunboat navy* (Columbia, 1993)

Turner, W., *British generals in the War of 1812: high command in the Canadas* (Montreal, 1999)

Updike, F *The diplomacy of the War of 1812* (Baltimore, 1915)

Whitehorn, J *While Washington burned: the battle for Fort Erie* (Baltimore, 1992)

Whitehorn, J *The battle of Baltimore* (Baltimore, 1997)

Wilder, P *The battle of Sackett's Harbour* (Annapolis, 1994)

Zaslow, M (ed) *The defended border: Upper Canada and the War of 1812* (Toronto, 1964)

Index